RAINER MARIA RILKE

RAINER MARIA RILKE was born in Prague in 1875, the son of an Austrian army officer. He studied at Prague, Munich, and Berlin, and published his first collection of poems, *Leben und Lieder*, in 1898. Rilke resisted all efforts to have them reprinted and they are today undiscoverable. Two other collections of poems were published in 1898, *Larenopfer* and *Traumgekront*. This was the year when he made his first trip to Italy and in the following year he went to Russia and met Tolstoi, whose influence can be clearly seen in *Die Geschichten vom Lieben Gott* (*Stories of God*). At Worpswede where Rilke lived for a time, he met and married Clara Westhoff, who had been a pupil of Rodin. He became the friend, and for a time the secretary, of Rodin when he moved to Paris, and it was during his twelve-year Paris residence, which lasted till July 1914, that Rilke's greatest poetic activity occurred. His first great work, *Das Stundenbuch*, appeared in 1906, followed in 1907 by *Neue Gedichte* and *Die Aufzeichnungen des Malte Laurids Brigge*. He continued to travel, to Italy, Spain, Egypt, and Sweden, but always returned to Paris.

When World War I broke out, he was obliged to leave France and during the War he lived in Munich. In 1919 he went to Switzerland where he spent the last years of his life. It was here that he wrote his last two works, the *Sonnets to Orpheus* and the *Duino Elegies*. He died on December 29, 1926. At the time of his death his work was intensely admired by many leading artists of Europe, including Gide, Valéry, and Stefan Zweig, but was almost unknown to the general reading public. His reputation, like that of Proust (who died during the same year) has grown steadily since his death, and he has come to be regarded as a modern German classic.

RAINER MARIA RILKE

In Translations by M. D. HERTER NORTON
Letters to a Young Poet
Sonnets to Orpheus
Wartime Letters of Rainer Maria Rilke
Translations from the Poetry of Rainer Maria Rilke
The Tale of the Love and Death of Cornet Christopher Rilke
The Notebooks of Malte Laurids Brigge

Translated by M. D. HERTER NORTON and NORA PURTSCHER-
WYDENBRUCK
Stories of God

Translated by STEPHEN SPENDER and J. B. LEISHMAN
Duino Elegies

Translated by JANE BANNARD GREENE and M D. HERTER NORTON
Letters of Rainer Maria Rilke
Volume One, 1892–1910   Volume Two, 1910–1926

SONNETS TO ORPHEUS

by
Rainer Maria Rilke

Translated by
M. D. HERTER NORTON

The Norton Library
W·W·NORTON & COMPANY·INC·
NEW YORK

FIRST PUBLISHED IN THE NORTON LIBRARY 1962

W. W. Norton & Company, Inc. is also the publisher
of *The Norton Anthology of English Literature,* edited by M. H.
Abrams, Robert M. Adams, David Daiches, E. Talbot Donaldson,
George H. Ford, Samuel Holt Monk, and Hallet Smith; *The American
Tradition in Literature,* edited by Sculley Bradley, Richmond Croom
Beatty, and E. Hudson Long; *World Masterpieces,* edited by Maynard
Mack, Kenneth Douglas, Howard E. Hugo, Bernard M. W. Knox,
John C. McGalliard, P. M. Pasinetti, and René Wellek; and other
fine anthologies.

PRINTED IN THE UNITED STATES OF AMERICA

Contents

Foreword

To Rilke himself the *Sonnets to Orpheus* were "perhaps the most mysterious . . . in the way they came up and entrusted themselves to me, the most enigmatic dictation I have ever held through and achieved; the whole first part was written down in a single breathless act of obedience, between the 2nd and 5th of February, without one word being doubtful or having to be changed. And this at a time when I had prepared myself for another big work and was already busy with that too. How should one not increase in reverence and infinite gratitude over such experiences in one's own existence?"

The second part of the *Sonnets* was done by the 20th of the same month, the other big work, the *Duino Elegies,* of which the *Sonnets* were "in a way the natural overflow", were completed on the 11th, and betweenwhiles sundry late and fragmentary poems had also come into being. Well might the maker of all these exclaim, "February 1922 was my big time!"

The poems themselves are their own best reason for their title. Orpheus—the mythical poet, sometimes called the son of Apollo, who could enchant beasts and birds and spirits with his

song and might have brought back his Eurydice from the world
of the dead, had he not turned to look ere she had once more
set foot in the world of the living; Orpheus, singer of the known
and unknown, the visible and invisible, of being and not-being,
who was at home in both those realms which Rilke imagines
should, in the fullest consciousness of our existence, become
one—in what other symbol than that of poetry's own voice
should he have projected his understanding of man's final in-
terests, life and death?

But we look also for some more concrete impulse for the
inspiration of the *Sonnets,* and to this the subtitle gives the clue.
Rilke had spent the evening of New Year's Day reading an
account of the untimely death of the young daughter of friends,
sent him by the girl's mother, and he tells his publisher,
shortly after their completion, how the *Sonnets* seemed, more
and more as the work went on, to attach themselves to this
vanished figure; two—the next-to-last in each part—actually
refer to her, but many others hover about the connection. Also,
visitors to the Château de Muzot, the little twelfth-century stone
tower in Switzerland's Valais, where he was working through
his first solitary winter, would have seen hanging in the dining-
room window soffit a small engraving, representing Orpheus
with his lyre, which Rilke had chanced upon in a shop window,
and around which, he said, the *Sonnets* had in a flash grouped
themselves, taking its name, and leading thence to the thought
of a memorial to this girl who had died young. Yet behind these
more objective promptings that helped touch off the creative

storm, it is in the inner preoccupations of the poet's mind, as we read them through all his work, that we might more truly trace the genesis of this series of poems in which culminates the lyric output of a lifetime.

* * * *

In this first half of our century we have acquired a high regard for commentaries, so busying ourselves with what someone else has to say about a work of art that we have no eyesight left to look upon the work itself; we fear, perhaps, to trust our own understanding, and in so doing close off our individual freedom of imagination. In poetry's case we are driven to this in part by obscurities of allusion, but in part it happens because we are too anxious to get everything out of a poem at the first reading. But we cannot take it all in at once. The nature of its value undergoes change: now it is new, perhaps uncomfortable and difficult, anon it takes its place in our familiar world, and now again it has passed into our heritage and we enjoy it without effort. Rilke says himself that the *Sonnets to Orpheus* "may now and then confront the reader with some lack of consideration", and quite reasonably expects that much in them "might be difficult to grasp without a knowledge of certain assumptions and incidentally some familiarity with my attitude towards love and death". If one believes that the poet should be allowed to speak for himself to the greatest possible extent, such familiarity is perhaps best achieved from the reading of Rilke's works and of his letters.

In the Notes at the end of this volume I have attempted to include, besides the very few specific indications Rilke himself set down, some examples of relevant quotations from letters and some parallel passages in other poems, such as the *Duino Elegies,* which are so closely allied to the *Sonnets* in origin. These are far from exhaustive; on the contrary, I believe the reader derives a keener interest and satisfaction from those recognitions he comes upon in his own explorings than from mere rediscovery of what has been indicated to him. The document that, so far as I know, best states the principal larger concepts behind Rilke's thought and imagery in the *Sonnets,* as in the *Elegies,* is the letter to his Polish translator, quoted at some length in the Notes, which was not written, it is true, until three and a half years after the poetry, with whatever that may imply of afterthought. To attempt to read into this statement a whole metaphysical scheme into which everything Rilke ever said should fit would be far from the spirit of the *Sonnets,* as indeed of Rilke's intention generally. He had no use for "that sort of systematization". It may be said of poets, as Mr. Whitehead says of ancient writers, that while their systematic thought "is now nearly worthless . . . their detached insights are priceless".

Perhaps this appears like an evasion of responsibility on the translator's part, a confession that a difficult task of "interpretation" has been shirked. For interpretations may be suggestive, even if they often put a strain on the original. To a lady who sought to understand one of the *Sonnets* by calling upon the idea of the transmigration of souls, Rilke wrote: "You are think-

ing too far out beyond the poem itself. . . . I believe that no
poem in the Sonnets to Orpheus means anything that is not
fully written out there, often, it is true, with its most secret name.
All 'allusion' I am convinced would be contradictory to the
indescribable 'being-there' of the poem." The translator's prime
effort has gone into the translation itself, into the search for
equivalents—not dictionary equivalents, but those that should
take in the special flavor, the corresponding ambiguity, the
poet's usage, the "secret name". I still believe that the closest
adherence to the poetry itself is best achieved through the most
literal possible rendering of word, phrase, image, far as the result
may prove to remain from the final perfection, the "indescrib-
able 'being-there' " of the original poem.

> "When *I* use a word," Humpty Dumpty said in rather a
> scornful tone, "it means just what I choose it to mean—
> neither more nor less."
> "The question is," said Alice, "whether you *can* make
> words mean so many different things."
> "The question is," said Humpty Dumpty, "which is to be
> master—that's all."

*   *   *   *

Once more my thanks go to Frieda Planck Clarke, of River-
dale, New York, Philip Clark Horton, of Cambridge, Massa-
chusetts, Hermann Weyl, of Princeton, New Jersey, and this
time also to Herbert Steiner, of Zurich, the editor of *Corona,*
who is now in this country. Without the interest and help of

these good friends the translation would not approach even so nearly as it may the unachievable goal of translators of Rilke.

New York,
April 21, 1942.

The Sonnets to Orpheus

written as a monument

for

Vera Ouckama Knoop

⅃⅃⅃⅃⅃⅃⅃⅃

CHATEAU DE MUZOT

FEBRUARY

1922

First Part

1

Dₐ stieg ein Baum. O reine Übersteigung!
O Orpheus singt! O hoher Baum im Ohr!
Und alles schwieg. Doch selbst in der Verschweigung
ging neuer Anfang, Wink und Wandlung vor.

Tiere aus Stille drangen aus dem klaren
gelösten Wald von Lager und Genist;
und da ergab sich, dass sie nicht aus List
und nicht aus Angst in sich so leise waren,

sondern aus Hören. Brüllen, Schrei, Geröhr
schien klein in ihren Herzen. Und wo eben
kaum eine Hütte war, dies zu empfangen,

ein Unterschlupf aus dunkelstem Verlangen
mit einem Zugang, dessen Pfosten beben,—
da schufst du ihnen Tempel im Gehör.

1

THERE rose a tree. O pure transcendency!
O Orpheus singing! O tall tree in the ear!
And all was silent. Yet even in the silence
new beginning, beckoning, change went on.

Creatures of stillness thronged out of the clear
released wood from lair and nesting-place;
and it turned out that not from cunning and not
from fear were they so hushed within themselves,

but from harkening. Bellow and cry and roar
seemed little in their hearts. And where before
hardly a hut had been to take this in,

a covert out of darkest longing
with an entrance way whose timbers tremble,—
you built temples for them in their hearing.

2

Und fast ein Mädchen wars und ging hervor
aus diesem einigen Glück von Sang und Leier
und glänzte klar durch ihre Frühlingsschleier
und machte sich ein Bett in meinem Ohr.

Und schlief in mir. Und alles war ihr Schlaf.
Die Bäume, die ich je bewundert, diese
fühlbare Ferne, die gefühlte Wiese
und jedes Staunen, das mich selbst betraf.

Sie schlief die Welt. Singender Gott, wie hast
du sie vollendet, dass sie nicht begehrte,
erst wach zu sein? Sieh, sie erstand und schlief.

Wo ist ihr Tod? O, wirst du dies Motiv
erfinden noch, eh sich dein Lied verzehrte?—
Wo sinkt sie hin aus mir? . . . Ein Mädchen fast . . .

2

ALMOST a girl it was and issued forth
from this concordant joy of song and lyre,
and clearly shining through her springtime veils
she made herself a bed inside my ear.

And slept in me. And all things were her sleep.
The trees I always marveled at, those
feelable distances, the meadow felt
and every wondering that befell myself.

She slept the world. You singing god, how
did you so perfect her that she did not crave
first to be awake? See, she arose and slept.

Where is her death? O will you yet invent
this theme before your song consumes itself?—
Whither is she sinking out of me? . . . A girl almost . . .

3

*E*IN Gott vermags. Wie aber, sag mir, soll
ein Mann ihm folgen durch die schmale Leier?
Sein Sinn ist Zwiespalt. An der Kreuzung zweier
Herzwege steht kein Tempel für Apoll.

Gesang, wie du ihn lehrst, ist nicht Begehr,
nicht Werbung um ein endlich noch Erreichtes;
Gesang ist Dasein. Für den Gott ein Leichtes.
Wann aber *sind* wir? Und wann wendet er

an unser Sein die Erde und die Sterne?
Dies *ists* nicht, Jüngling, dass du liebst, wenn auch
die Stimme dann den Mund dir aufstösst,—lerne

vergessen dass du aufsangst. Das verrinnt.
In Wahrheit singen, ist ein andrer Hauch.
Ein Hauch um nichts. Ein Wehn im Gott. Ein Wind.

3

A god can do it. But how, tell me, shall
a man follow him through the narrow lyre?
His mind is cleavage. At the crossing of two
heartways stands no temple for Apollo.

Song, as you teach it, is not desire,
not suing for something yet in the end attained;
song is existence. Easy for the god.
But when do we *exist*? And when does he

spend the earth and stars upon our being?
Youth, this is not it, your loving, even
if then your voice thrusts your mouth open,—learn

to forget your sudden song. That will run out.
Real singing is a different breath.
A breath for nothing. A wafting in the god. A wind.

4

O ihr Zärtlichen, tretet zuweilen
in den Atem, der euch nicht meint,
lasst ihn an eueren Wangen sich teilen,
hinter euch zittert er, wieder vereint.

O ihr Seligen, o ihr Heilen,
die ihr der Anfang der Herzen scheint.
Bogen der Pfeile und Ziele von Pfeilen,
ewiger glänzt euer Lächeln verweint.

Fürchtet euch nicht zu leiden, die Schwere,
gebt sie zurück an der Erde Gewicht;
schwer sind die Berge, schwer sind die Meere.

Selbst die als Kinder ihr pflanztet, die Bäume,
wurden zu schwer längst; ihr trüget sie nicht.
Aber die Lüfte . . . aber die Räume . . .

4

O you tender ones, step now and then
into the breath that takes no heed of you;
let it part as it touches your cheeks,
it will quiver behind you, united again.

O you who are blessed, o you who are whole,
you who seem the beginning of hearts.
Bows for the arrows and targets of arrows,
tear-stained your smile shines more everlasting.

Fear not suffering; the heaviness,
give it back to the weight of the earth;
the mountains are heavy, heavy the oceans.

Even the trees you planted as children
long since grew too heavy, you could not sustain them.
Ah, but the breezes . . . ah, but the spaces . . .

5

Errichtet keinen Denkstein. Lasst die Rose
nur jedes Jahr zu seinen Gunsten blühn.
Denn Orpheus ists. Seine Metamorphose
in dem und dem. Wir sollen uns nicht mühn

um andre Namen. Ein für alle Male
ists Orpheus, wenn es singt. Er kommt und geht.
Ists nicht schon viel, wenn er die Rosenschale
um ein paar Tage manchmal übersteht?

O wie er schwinden muss, dass ihrs begrifft!
Und wenn ihm selbst auch bangte, dass er schwände.
Indem sein Wort das Hiersein übertrifft,

ist er schon dort, wohin ihrs nicht begleitet.
Der Leier Gitter zwängt ihm nicht die Hände.
Und er gehorcht, indem er überschreitet.

5

Set up no stone to his memory.
Just let the rose bloom each year for his sake.
For it is Orpheus. His metamorphosis
in this one and in this. We should not trouble

about other names. Once and for all
it's Orpheus when there's singing. He comes and goes.
Is it not much already if at times
he overstays for a few days the bowl of roses?

O how he has to vanish, for you to grasp it!
Though he himself take fright at vanishing.
Even while his word transcends the being-here,

he's there already where you do not follow.
The lyre's lattice does not snare his hands.
And he obeys, while yet he oversteps.

6

*I*ST er ein Hiesiger? Nein, aus beiden
Reichen erwuchs seine weite Natur.
Kundiger böge die Zweige der Weiden,
wer die Wurzeln der Weiden erfuhr.

Geht ihr zu Bette, so lasst auf dem Tische
Brot nicht und Milch nicht; die Toten ziehts—.
Aber er, der Beschwörende, mische
unter der Milde des Augenlids

ihre Erscheinung in alles Geschaute;
und der Zauber von Erdrauch und Raute
sei ihm so wahr wie der klarste Bezug.

Nichts kann das gültige Bild ihm verschlimmern;
sei es aus Gräbern, sei es aus Zimmern,
rühme er Fingerring, Spange und Krug.

6

Does he belong here? No, out of both
realms his wide nature grew.
More knowing would he bend the willows' branches
who has experienced the willows' roots.

Going to bed, leave on the table
no bread and no milk; it draws the dead—.
But he, the conjuror, let him
under the eyelid's mildness

mix their appearance into everything seen;
and may the magic of earthsmoke and rue
be to him as true as the clearest relation.

Nothing can harm for him the valid symbol;
be it from graves, be it from rooms,
let him praise finger-ring, clasp and jug.

7

Rühmen, das ists! Ein zum Rühmen Bestellter,
ging er hervor wie das Erz aus des Steins
Schweigen. Sein Herz, o vergängliche Kelter
eines den Menschen unendlichen Weins.

Nie versagt ihm die Stimme am Staube,
wenn ihn das göttliche Beispiel ergreift.
Alles wird Weinberg, alles wird Traube,
in seinem fühlenden Süden gereift.

Nicht in den Grüften der Könige Moder
straft ihm die Rühmung Lügen, oder
dass von den Göttern ein Schatten fällt.

Er ist einer der bleibenden Boten,
der noch weit in die Türen der Toten
Schalen mit rühmlichen Früchten hält.

7

PRAISING, that's it! One appointed to praising,
he came like the ore forth from the stone's
silence. His heart, o ephemeral press
of a wine that for men is unending.

His voice never flags in the dust,
when the godly example grips him.
Everything turns to vineyard, to grape,
ripened in his sentient South.

Not mold in the vaults of kings
gives the lie to his praising, nor
that a shadow falls from the gods.

He is one of the staying messengers,
who still holds far into the doors of the dead
bowls with fruits worthy of praise.

8

Nur im Raum der Rühmung darf die Klage
gehn, die Nymphe des geweinten Quells,
wachend über unserm Niederschlage,
dass er klar sei an demselben Fels,

der die Tore trägt und die Altäre.—
Sieh, um ihre stillen Schultern früht
das Gefühl, dass sie die jüngste wäre
unter den Geschwistern im Gemüt.

Jubel *weiss*, und Sehnsucht ist geständig,—
nur die Klage lernt noch; mädchenhändig
zählt sie nächtelang das alte Schlimme.

Aber plötzlich, schräg und ungeübt,
hält sie doch ein Sternbild unsrer Stimme
in den Himmel, den ihr Hauch nicht trübt.

8

O NLY in the realm of praising may Lament
go, nymph of the weeping spring,
watching over our precipitation,
that it be clear at the very rock

that bears the portals and the altars.—
See, round her still shoulders dawning hovers
the feeling that she is the youngest one
among the sister-moods in the spirit.

Jubilance *knows,* and Longing acquiesces,—
only Lament is learning still; with girlish hands
she reckons night on night the ancient evil.

Yet suddenly, aslant, unpracticed, even so
she holds a constellation of our voice
into the sky, unclouded by her breath.

9

Nur wer die Leier schon **hob**
auch unter Schatten,
darf das unendliche **Lob**
ahnend erstatten.

Nur wer mit Toten vom **Mohn**
ass, von dem ihren,
wird nicht den leisesten **Ton**
wieder verlieren.

Mag auch die Spieglung im **Teich**
oft uns verschwimmen:
Wisse das Bild.

Erst in dem Doppelbereich
werden die Stimmen
ewig und mild.

9

Oɴʟʏ one who has lifted the lyre
among shadows too,
may divining render
the infinite praise.

Only who with the dead has eaten
of the poppy that is theirs,
will never again lose
the most delicate tone.

Though the reflection in the pool
often swims before our eyes:
Know the image.

Only in the dual realm
do voices become
eternal and mild.

10

Euch, die ihr nie mein Gefühl verliesst,
grüss ich, antikische Sarkophage,
die das fröhliche Wasser römischer Tage
als ein wandelndes Lied durchfliesst.

Oder jene so offenen, wie das Aug
eines frohen erwachenden Hirten,
—innen voll Stille und Bienensaug—
denen entzückte Falter entschwirrten;

alle, die man dem Zweifel entreisst,
grüss ich, die wiedergeöffneten Munde,
die schon wussten, was schweigen heisst.

Wissen wirs, Freunde, wissen wirs nicht?
Beides bildet die zögernde Stunde
in dem menschlichen Angesicht.

10

You, who have never left my feeling,
I greet, antique sarcophagi,
whom the happy waters of Roman days
flow through as a wandering song.

Or those so open, like the eyes
of a happy awakening shepherd,
—full of stillness within and bee-balm—
whence flittered enchanted butterflies;

all those whom one wrests from doubt
I greet, the mouths once again opened
that already knew what silence means.

Do we know it, friends, do we not know it?
These two mold the hesitant hour
in the countenance of man.

11

S<small>IEH</small> den Himmel. Heisst kein Sternbild „Reiter"?
Denn dies ist uns seltsam eingeprägt:
dieser Stolz aus Erde. Und ein zweiter,
der ihn treibt und hält und den er trägt.

Ist nicht so, gejagt und dann gebändigt,
diese sehnige Natur des Seins?
Weg und Wendung. Doch ein Druck verständigt.
Neue Weite. Und die zwei sind eins.

Aber *sind* sie's? Oder meinen beide
nicht den Weg, den sie zusammen tun?
Namenlos schon trennt sie Tisch und Weide.

Auch die sternische Verbindung trügt.
Doch uns freue eine Weile nun,
der Figur zu glauben. Das genügt.

11

Sᴇᴇ the sky. Is there no constellation
called "Rider"? For this is strangely impressed
on us: this earthy pride. And a second,
who drives and holds it and whom it bears.

Is not the sinewy nature of our being
just like this, spurred on and then reined in?
Track and turning. Yet at a touch, understanding.
New open spaces. And the two are one.

But *are* they? Or do both not mean
the way they take together? Already
table and pasture utterly divide them.

Even the starry union is deceptive.
But let us now be glad a while
to believe the figure. That's enough.

12

Heil dem Geist, der uns verbinden mag;
denn wir leben wahrhaft in Figuren.
Und mit kleinen Schritten gehn die Uhren
neben unserm eigentlichen Tag.

Ohne unsern wahren Platz zu kennen,
handeln wir aus wirklichem Bezug.
Die Antennen fühlen die Antennen,
und die leere Ferne trug . . .

Reine Spannung. O Musik der Kräfte!
Ist nicht durch die lässlichen Geschäfte
jede Störung von dir abgelenkt?

Selbst wenn sich der Bauer sorgt und handelt,
wo die Saat in Sommer sich verwandelt,
reicht er niemals hin. Die Erde *schenkt*.

12

HAIL to the spirit that can unite us;
for we do truly live in figures.
And with little steps the clocks go on
alongside our essential day.

Without knowing our true place,
we act out of real relationship.
Antennae feel antennae,
and the empty distance bore . . .

Pure tension. O music of the forces!
Are not all disturbances deflected
from you by our casual occupations?

No matter if the farmer works and worries,
where the seed is turning into summer
he never reaches. The earth *bestows*.

13

Voller Apfel, Birne und Banane,
Stachelbeere . . . Alles dieses spricht
Tod und Leben in den Mund . . . Ich ahne . . .
Lest es einem Kind vom Angesicht,

wenn es sie erschmeckt. Dies kommt von weit.
Wird euch langsam namenlos im Munde?
Wo sonst Worte waren, fliessen Funde,
aus dem Fruchtfleisch überrascht befreit.

Wagt zu sagen, was ihr Apfel nennt.
Diese Süsse, die sich erst verdichtet,
um, im Schmecken leise aufgerichtet,

klar zu werden, wach und transparent,
doppeldeutig, sonnig, erdig, hiesig—:
O Erfahrung, Fühlung, Freude—, riesig!

13

Full round apple, pear and banana,
gooseberry . . . All this speaks
death and life into the mouth . . . I sense . . .
Read it from the face of a child

tasting them. This comes from far. Is something
indescribable slowly happening in your mouth?
Where otherwise words were, flow discoveries,
freed all surprised out of the fruit's flesh.

Dare to say what you call apple. This
sweetness, first concentrating, that it may,
in the tasting delicately raised,

grow clear, awake, transparent, double-meaning'd,
sunny, earthy, of the here and now—:
O experience, sensing, joy—, immense!

14

Wɪʀ gehen um mit Blume, Weinblatt, Frucht.
Sie sprechen nicht die Sprache nur des Jahres.
Aus Dunkel steigt ein buntes Offenbares
und hat vielleicht den Glanz der Eifersucht

der Toten an sich, die die Erde stärken.
Was wissen wir von ihrem Teil an dem?
Es ist seit lange ihre Art, den Lehm
mit ihrem freien Marke zu durchmärken.

Nun fragt sich nur: tun sie es gern? . . .
Drängt diese Frucht, ein Werk von schweren Sklaven,
geballt zu uns empor, zu ihren Herrn?

Sind *sie* die Herrn, die bei den Wurzeln schlafen,
und gönnen uns aus ihren Überflüssen
dies Zwischending aus stummer Kraft und Küssen?

14

WE have to do with flower, vine-leaf, fruit.
They speak the language not only of the year.
Out of darkness rises a motley manifest,
having perhaps the gleam of the jealousy

of the dead about it, who invigorate the earth.
What do we know of their share in this?
It has long been their way to marrow the loam
through and through with their free marrow.

The only question: do they do it gladly?
Does this fruit, a work of heavy slaves,
push up, clenched, to us, to their masters?

Are *they* the masters, who sleep with the roots,
and grant to us out of their overflow
this hybrid thing made of dumb strength and kisses?

15

Wartet . . . , das schmeckt . . . Schon ists auf der Flucht.
. . . Wenig Musik nur, ein Stampfen, ein Summen—:
Mädchen, ihr warmen, Mädchen, ihr stummen,
tanzt den Geschmack der erfahrenen Frucht!

Tanzt die Orange. Wer kann sie vergessen,
wie sie, ertrinkend in sich, sich wehrt
wider ihr Süßsein. Ihr habt sie besessen.
Sie hat sich köstlich zu euch bekehrt.

Tanzt die Orange. Die wärmere Landschaft,
werft sie aus euch, dass die reife erstrahle
in Lüften der Heimat! Erglühte, enthüllt

Düfte um Düfte! Schafft die Verwandtschaft
mit der reinen, sich weigernden Schale,
mit dem Saft, der die glückliche füllt!

15

W<small>AIT</small> . . . , that tastes good . . . It's already in flight.
. . . Just a little music, a stamping, a humming—:
Girls, you warm, you silent girls,
dance the taste of the fruit experienced!

Dance the orange. Who can forget it,
how, drowning in itself, it resists
its being-sweet. You have possessed it.
It has been deliciously converted to you.

Dance the orange. The warmer landscape,
fling it out of you, that the ripe one be radiant
in homeland breezes! Aglow, peel away

perfume on perfume! Create the relation
with the pure, reluctant rind,
with the juice that fills the happy fruit!

16

Du, mein Freund, bist einsam, weil ...
Wir machen mit Worten und Fingerzeigen
uns allmählich die Welt zu eigen,
vielleicht ihren schwächsten, gefährlichsten **Teil**.

Wer zeigt mit Fingern auf einen Geruch?—
Doch von den Kräften, die uns bedrohten,
fühlst du viele ... Du kennst die Toten,
und du erschrickst vor dem Zauberspruch.

Sieh, nun heisst es zusammen ertragen
Stückwerk und Teile, als sei es das Ganze.
Dir helfen, wird schwer sein. Vor allem: pflanze

mich nicht in dein Herz. Ich wüchse zu schnell.
Doch *meines* Herrn Hand will ich führen und sagen:
Hier. Das ist Esau in seinem Fell.

16

You, my friend, are lonely, because . . .
We, with words and finger-pointings,
gradually make the world our own,
perhaps its weakest, most precarious part.

Who points with fingers to a smell?—
Yet of the powers that threaten us
you feel many . . . You know the dead,
and you shrink away from the magic spell.

See, now we two together must bear
piece-work and parts as though it were the whole.
Helping you will be hard. Above all, do not

plant me in your heart. I should grow too fast.
But I will guide *my* master's hand and say:
Here. This is Esau in his pelt.

17

Zu unterst der Alte, verworrn,
all der Erbauten
Wurzel, verborgener Born,
den sie nie schauten.

Sturmhelm und Jägerhorn,
Spruch von Ergrauten,
Männer im Bruderzorn,
Frauen wie Lauten . . .

Drängender Zweig an Zweig,
nirgends ein freier . . .
Einer! o steig . . . o steig . . .

Aber sie brechen noch.
Dieser erst oben doch
biegt sich zur Leier.

17

*NDERMOST the Ancient, entangled,
root of all those
upreared, concealed source
they never saw.

Helmet and hunter's horn,
saying of graybeards,
men in their brother-wrath,
women like lutes . . .

Branch crowding on branch,
not one of them free . . .
One! o climb . . . o climb . . .

But still they break.
Yet this top one at last
bends into a lyre.

18

Hörst du das Neue, Herr,
dröhnen und beben?
Kommen Verkündiger,
die es erheben.

Zwar ist kein Hören heil
in dem Durchtobtsein,
doch der Maschinenteil
will jetzt gelobt sein.

Sieh, die Maschine:
wie sie sich wälzt und rächt
und uns entstellt und schwächt.

Hat sie aus uns auch Kraft,
sie, ohne Leidenschaft,
treibe und diene.

18

*M*ASTER, do you hear the New,
droning and throbbing?
Harbingers come,
those who exalt it.

True, no hearing is whole
in all the turmoil,
yet the machine-part
now wants to be praised.

See, the machine:
how it wallows and wreaks revenge,
distorts and weakens us.

Though it has strength from us,
let it, dispassionate,
drive and serve.

19

Wandelt sich rasch auch die Welt
wie Wolkengestalten,
alles Vollendete fällt
heim zum Uralten.

Über dem Wandel und Gang,
weiter und freier,
währt noch dein Vor-Gesang,
Gott mit der Leier.

Nicht sind die Leiden erkannt,
nicht ist die Liebe gelernt,
und was im Tod uns entfernt,

ist nicht entschleiert.
Einzig das Lied überm Land
heiligt und feiert.

19

E VEN though the world keeps changing
quickly as cloud-shapes,
all things perfected fall
home to the age-old.

Over the changing and passing,
wider and freer,
still lasts your leading-song,
god with the lyre.

Not understood are the sufferings.
Neither has love been learned,
and what removes us in death

is not unveiled.
Only song over the land
hallows and celebrates.

20

D IR aber, Herr, o was weih ich dir, sag,
der das Ohr den Geschöpfen gelehrt?—
Mein Erinnern an einen Frühlingstag,
seinen Abend, in Russland—, ein Pferd . . .

Herüber vom Dorf kam der Schimmel allein,
an der vorderen Fessel den Pflock,
um die Nacht auf den Wiesen allein zu sein;
wie schlug seiner Mähne Gelock

an den Hals im Takte des Übermuts,
bei dem grob gehemmten Galopp.
Wie sprangen die Quellen des Rossebluts!

Der fühlte die Weiten, und ob!
der sang und der hörte—, dein Sagenkreis
war *in* ihm geschlossen.

                    Sein Bild: ich weih's.

20

*B*UT what shall I dedicate to you, master, say,
who taught the creatures their ear?—
My memory of a day in Spring,
its evening, in Russia—, a horse . . .

Across from the village came the white horse alone,
on one fore fetlock the hobble,
to be alone for the night on the meadows;
how his shock of mane beat

on his neck in time with his high-mettled spirit,
in that rudely obstructed gallop.
How the springs of his steed's blood leapt!

That horse felt the distances, and how
he sang and heard!—your cycle of myths
was closed in him.
                              His image—I dedicate.

21

Frühling ist wiedergekommen. Die Erde
ist wie ein Kind, das Gedichte weiss;
viele, o viele . . . Für die Beschwerde
langen Lernens bekommt sie den Preis.

Streng war ihr Lehrer. Wir mochten das Weisse
an dem Barte des alten Manns.
Nun, wie das Grüne, das Blaue heisse,
dürfen wir fragen: sie kanns, sie kanns!

Erde, die frei hat, du glückliche, spiele
nun mit den Kindern. Wir wollen dich fangen,
fröhliche Erde. Dem Frohsten gelingts.

O, was der Lehrer sie lehrte, das Viele,
und was gedruckt steht in Wurzeln und langen
schwierigen Stämmen: sie singts, sie singts!

21

Spring has come again. The earth
is like a child that knows poems by heart,
many, o many . . . For the vexation
of long learning she gets the prize.

Her teacher was strict. We liked the white
in the old man's beard.
And now we may ask what the green, the blue
is called: she knows it, she knows!

Earth, having holiday, lucky earth, play
now with the children. We want to catch you,
happy earth. The happiest will succeed.

O, what her teacher taught her, the many things,
and what stands printed in roots and long
difficult stems: she sings it, she sings!

22

WIR sind die Treibenden.
Aber den Schritt der Zeit,
nehmt ihn als Kleinigkeit
im immer Bleibenden.

Alles das Eilende
wird schon vorüber sein;
denn das Verweilende
erst weiht uns ein.

Knaben, o werft den Mut
nicht in die Schnelligkeit,
nicht in den Flugversuch.

Alles ist ausgeruht:
Dunkel und Helligkeit,
Blume und Buch.

22

*W*E are the driving ones.
O but the stride of time,
take it as trifle
in the ever remaining.

All that is hurrying
will already be over;
for first the abiding
initiates us.

Boys, o fling your courage
not into speediness,
not into flight-trials.

All these are rested:
darkness and light,
flower and book.

23

Oerst *dann,* wenn der Flug
nicht mehr um seinetwillen
wird in die Himmelsstillen
steigen, sich selber genug,

um in lichten Profilen,
als das Gerät, das gelang,
Liebling der Winde zu spielen,
sicher schwenkend und schlank,—

erst wenn ein reines Wohin
wachsender Apparate
Knabenstolz überwiegt,

wird, überstürzt von Gewinn,
jener den Fernen Genahte
sein, was er einsam erfliegt.

23

O not till the time when flight
no longer will mount for its own sake
into the sky stillnesses,
sufficient unto itself,

that in luminous profilings,
as the tool that succeeded,
it may play the winds' favorite,
surely curving and slim,—

not till a pure whither
outweighs boyish pride
of growing machines,

will, headlong with winning,
one who has neared the distances
be his lone flight's attaining.

24

Sollen wir unsere uralte Freundschaft, die grossen
niemals werbenden Götter, weil sie der harte
Stahl, den wir streng erzogen, nicht kennt, verstossen
oder sie plötzlich suchen auf einer Karte?

Diese gewaltigen Freunde, die uns die Toten
nehmen, rühren nirgends an unsere Räder.
Unsere Gastmähler haben wir weit—, unsere Bäder,
fortgerückt, und ihre uns lang schon zu langsamen Boten

überholen wir immer. Einsamer nun aufeinander
ganz angewiesen, ohne einander zu kennen,
führen wir nicht mehr die Pfade als schöne Mäander,

sondern als Grade. Nur noch in Dampfkesseln brennen
die einstigen Feuer und heben die Hämmer, die immer
grössern. Wir aber nehmen an Kraft ab, wie Schwimmer.

24

SHALL we reject our age-old friendship, the great
never-soliciting gods, because the hard
steel we have strictly schooled does not know them,
or shall we suddenly seek them on a map?

These powerful friends, who take the dead
from us, nowhere touch against our wheels.
We have removed our banquets, our baths, afar,
and their messengers, long since too slow for us,

we always overtake. Lonelier now, wholly dependent
on one another, without knowing one another,
we no longer lay out the paths as lovely meanders,

but straight. Only in boilers now do the former
fires still burn, heaving the hammers that grow
always bigger. But we, we diminish in strength, like swimmers.

25

Dᴵᴄʜ aber will ich nun, dich, die ich kannte
wie eine Blume, von der ich den Namen nicht weiss,
noch *ein* Mal erinnern und ihnen zeigen, Entwandte,
schöne Gespielin des unüberwindlichen Schreis.

Tänzerin erst, die plötzlich, den Körper voll Zögern,
anhielt, als göss man ihr Jungsein in Erz;
trauernd und lauschend—. Da, von den hohen Vermögern
fiel ihr Musik in das veränderte Herz.

Nah war die Krankheit. Schon von den Schatten bemächtigt,
drängte verdunkelt das Blut, doch, wie flüchtig verdächtigt,
trieb es in seinen natürlichen Frühling hervor.

Wieder und wieder, von Dunkel und Sturz unterbrochen,
glänzte es irdisch. Bis es nach schrecklichem Pochen
trat in das trostlos offene Tor.

25

*B*UT you now, you whom I knew like a flower whose name
I don't know, I will *once* more remember and show you
to them, you who were taken away,
beautiful playmate of the invincible cry.

Dancer first, who suddenly, with body full of lingering,
paused, as though her youngness were being cast in bronze;
mourning and listening—. Then, from the high achievers
music fell into her altered heart.

Sickness was near. Already overcome by the shadows,
her blood pulsed more darkly, yet, as if fleetingly
suspect, it thrust forth into its natural spring.

Again and again, interrupted by darkness and downfall,
it gleamed of the earth. Until after terrible throbbing
it entered the hopelessly open portal.

26

Du aber, Göttlicher, du, bis zuletzt noch Ertöner,
da ihn der Schwarm der verschmähten Mänaden befiel,
hast ihr Geschrei übertönt mit Ordnung, du Schöner,
aus den Zerstörenden stieg dein erbauendes Spiel.

Keine war da, dass sie Haupt dir und Leier zerstör',
wie sie auch rangen und rasten; und alle die scharfen
Steine, die sie nach deinem Herzen warfen,
wurden zu Sanftem an dir und begabt mit Gehör.

Schliesslich zerschlugen sie dich, von der Rache gehetzt,
während dein Klang noch in Löwen und Felsen verweilte
und in den Bäumen und Vögeln. Dort singst du noch jetzt.

O du verlorener Gott! Du unendliche Spur!
Nur weil dich reissend zuletzt die Feindschaft verteilte,
sind wir die Hörenden jetzt und ein Mund der Natur.

26

*B*UT you, divine one, you, till the end still sounding,
when beset by the swarm of disdainèd maenads,
you outsounded their cries with order, beautiful one,
from among the destroyers arose your upbuilding music.

None of them there could destroy your head or your lyre,
however they wrestled and raged; and all the sharp
stones they flung at your heart
turned soft on touching you and gifted with hearing.

In the end they battered and broke you, harried by vengeance,
the while your resonance lingered in lions and rocks
and in the trees and birds. There you are singing still.

O you lost god! You unending trace!
Only because at last enmity rent and scattered you
are we now the hearers and a mouth of Nature.

Second Part

1

Aᴛᴍᴇɴ, du unsichtbares Gedicht!
Immerfort um das eigne
Sein rein eingetauschter Weltraum. Gegengewicht,
in dem ich mich rhythmisch ereigne.

Einzige Welle, deren
allmähliches Meer ich bin;
sparsamstes du von allen möglichen Meeren,—
Raumgewinn.

Wie viele von diesen Stellen der Räume waren schon
innen in mir. Manche Winde
sind wie mein Sohn.

Erkennst du mich, Luft, du, voll noch einst meiniger Orte?
Du, einmal glatte Rinde,
Rundung und Blatt meiner Worte.

1

*REATHING, you invisible poem!
World-space constantly in pure
interchange with our own being. Counterpoise,
wherein I rhythmically happen.

Solitary wave,
whose gradual sea I am;
most sparing you of all possible seas,—
winning of space.

How many of these places in space have already been
within me. Many a wind
is like a son to me.

Do you know me, you air, still full of places once mine?
You onetime smooth rind,
rondure and leaf of my words.

2

So wie dem Meister manchmal das eilig
nähere Blatt den *wirklichen* Strich
abnimmt: so nehmen oft Spiegel das heilig
einzige Lächeln der Mädchen in sich,

wenn sie den Morgen erproben, allein,—
oder im Glanze der dienenden Lichter.
Und in das Atmen der echten Gesichter,
später, fällt nur ein Widerschein.

Was haben Augen einst ins umrusste
lange Verglühn der Kamine geschaut:
Blicke des Lebens, für immer verlorne.

Ach, der Erde, wer kennt die Verluste?
Nur, wer mit dennoch preisendem Laut
sänge das Herz, das ins Ganze geborne.

2

As sometimes the hurriedly nearer leaf
catches the *authentic* stroke from the master's
hand: so mirrors often take into themselves
the sacred single smile of girls,

when they assay the morning, alone,—
or in the gleam of the servient lights.
And into the breathing of their real faces,
later, only a reflection falls.

What have eyes once gazed into the charred
and slowly dying glow of fireplaces:
glances of life, forever lost.

The earth—ah, who knows her losses?
Only one who with nonetheless praising sound
would sing the heart, born into the whole.

3

Spiegel: noch nie hat man wissend beschrieben,
was ihr in euerem Wesen seid.
Ihr, wie mit lauter Löchern von Sieben
erfüllten Zwischenräume der Zeit.

Ihr, noch des leeren Saales Verschwender—,
wenn es dämmert, wie Wälder weit . . .
Und der Lüster geht wie ein Sechzehn-Ender
durch eure Unbetretbarkeit.

Manchmal seid ihr voll Malerei.
Einige scheinen *in* euch gegangen—,
andere schicktet ihr scheu vorbei.

Aber die Schönste wird bleiben, bis
drüben in ihre enthaltenen Wangen
eindrang der klare gelöste Narziss.

3

Mirrors: never yet has anyone described,
knowing, what you are really like.
You, interstices of time
filled as it were with nothing but sieveholes.

You, squanderers still of the empty hall—,
when dusk comes on, wide as the woods . . .
And the luster goes like a sixteen-pointer
through your impenetrability.

Sometimes you are full of painting.
A few seem to have gone *into* you—,
others you sent shyly by.

But the loveliest will remain, until in yonder
to her withheld cheeks the clear
released Narcissus penetrates.

4

O dieses ist das Tier, das es nicht gibt.
Sie wusstens nicht und habens jeden Falls
—sein Wandeln, seine Haltung, seinen Hals,
bis in des stillen Blickes Licht—geliebt.

Zwar *war* es nicht. Doch weil sie's liebten, ward
ein reines Tier. Sie liessen immer Raum.
Und in dem Raume, klar und ausgespart,
erhob es leicht sein Haupt und brauchte kaum

zu sein. Sie nährten es mit keinem Korn,
nur immer mit der Möglichkeit, es sei.
Und sie gab solche Stärke an das Tier,

dass es aus sich ein Stirnhorn trieb. Ein Horn.
Zu einer Jungfrau kam es weiss herbei—
und war im Silber-Spiegel und in ihr.

4

O this is the creature that does not exist.
They did not know that and in any case
—its motion, and its bearing, and its neck,
even to the light of its still gaze—they loved it.

Indeed it never *was*. Yet because they loved it,
a pure creature happened. They always allowed room.
And in that room, clear and left open,
it easily raised its head and scarcely needed

to be. They fed it with no grain, but ever
with the possibility that it might be.
And this gave the creature such strength,

it grew a horn out of its brow. One horn.
To a virgin it came hither white—
and was in the silver-mirror and in her.

5

B LUMENMUSKEL, der der Anemone
Wiesenmorgen nach und nach erschliesst,
bis in ihren Schooss das polyphone
Licht der lauten Himmel sich ergiesst,

in den stillen Blütenstern gespannter
Muskel des unendlichen Empfangs,
manchmal *so* von Fülle übermannter,
dass der Ruhewink des Untergangs

kaum vermag die weitzurückgeschnellten
Blätterränder dir zurückzugeben:
du, Entschluss und Kraft von *wieviel* Welten!

Wir Gewaltsamen, wir währen länger.
Aber *wann,* in welchem aller Leben,
sind wir endlich offen und Empfänger?

5

*F*LOWER-MUSCLE, that opens the anemone's
meadow-morning bit by bit,
until into her lap the polyphonic
light of the loud skies pours down,

muscle of infinite reception
tensed in the still star of the blossom,
sometimes *so* overmanned with abundance
that the sunset's beckoning to rest

is scarcely able to give back to you
the wide-sprung petal-edges:
you, resolve and strength of *how many* worlds!

We, with our violence, are longer-lasting.
But *when,* in which one of all lives,
are we at last open and receivers?

6

Rose, du thronende, denen im Altertume
warst du ein Kelch mit einfachem Rand.
Uns aber bist du die volle zahllose Blume,
der unerschöpfliche Gegenstand.

In deinem Reichtum scheinst du wie Kleidung um Kleidung
um einen Leib aus nichts als Glanz;
aber dein einzelnes Blatt ist zugleich die Vermeidung
und die Verleugnung jedes Gewands.

Seit Jahrhunderten ruft uns dein Duft
seine süssesten Namen herüber;
plötzlich liegt er wie Ruhm in der Luft.

Dennoch, wir wissen ihn nicht zu nennen, wir raten . . .
Und Erinnerung geht zu ihm über,
die wir von rufbaren Stunden erbaten.

6

Rose, you throning one, to them of ancient times
you were a chalice with a simple rim.
But for *us* you are the full, the countless flower,
the inexhaustible object.

In your richness you seem like raiment on raiment
about a body of nothing but light;
but your single leaf is at once the shunning
and the denial of all attire.

For centuries your fragrance has been calling
its sweetest names across to us;
suddenly it lies in the air like fame.

Even so, we don't know what to call it, we guess . . .
And memory goes over to it
that we have asked from hours we could call.

7

*B*LUMEN, ihr schliesslich den ordnenden Händen verwandte,
(Händen der Mädchen von einst und jetzt),
die auf dem Gartentisch oft von Kante zu Kante
lagen, ermattet und sanft verletzt,

wartend des Wassers, das sie noch einmal erhole
aus dem begonnenen Tod—, und nun
wieder erhobene zwischen die strömenden Pole
fühlender Finger, die wohlzutun

mehr noch vermögen, als ihr ahntet, ihr leichten,
wenn ihr euch wiederfandet im Krug,
langsam erkühlend und Warmes von Mädchen, wie Beichten,

von euch gebend, wie trübe ermüdende Sünden,
die das Gepflücktsein beging, als Bezug
wieder zu ihnen, die sich euch blühend verbünden.

7

*F*LOWERS, kin in the end to those arranging hands,
(girls' hands of then and now),
you that lay on the garden table often from edge
to edge, drooping and gently hurt,

awaiting the water that once more was to recover you
from death already begun—, and now
lifted again between the streaming poles
of feeling fingers that are able to do

even more good than you guessed, light ones,
when you came to yourselves in the pitcher,
slowly cooling and giving warmness of girls,

like confessions, from you, like dreary wearying sins
committed by your being plucked, relating you
again to those who are your allies in blooming.

8

Wenige ihr, der einstigen Kindheit Gespielen
in den zerstreuten Gärten der Stadt:
wie wir uns fanden und uns zögernd gefielen
und, wie das Lamm mit dem redenden Blatt,

sprachen als schweigende. Wenn wir uns einmal freuten,
keinem gehörte es. Wessen wars?
Und wie zergings unter allen den gehenden Leuten
und im Bangen des langen Jahrs.

Wagen umrollten uns fremd, vorübergezogen,
Häuser umstanden uns stark, aber unwahr,—und keines
kannte uns je. *Was* war wirklich im All?

Nichts. Nur die Bälle. Ihre herrlichen Bogen.
Auch nicht die Kinder . . . Aber manchmal trat eines,
ach ein vergehendes, unter den fallenden Ball.

In memoriam Egon von Rilke

8

O you few, playmates of onetime childhood
in the scattered gardens of the city:
how we found and shyly fancied one another
and, like the lamb with the speaking scroll,

spoke, being silent. Whenever we were glad,
it belonged to no one. Whose was it?
And how it melted away among all the walking people
and in the anxiety of the long year.

Carriages rolled round us indifferent, drawn past,
houses stood round us strong, but unreal,—and none of them
ever knew us. What *was* real in the All?

Nothing. Only the balls. Their glorious curves.
Not even the children . . . But sometimes one would step,
alas, ephemeral, under the falling ball.

In memoriam Egon von Rilke

9

Rühmt euch, ihr Richtenden, nicht der entbehrlichen Folter
und dass das Eisen nicht länger an Hälsen sperrt.
Keins ist gesteigert, kein Herz—, weil ein gewollter
Krampf der Milde euch zarter verzerrt.

Was es durch Zeiten bekam, das schenkt das Schafott
wieder zurück, wie Kinder ihr Spielzeug vom vorig
alten Geburtstag. Ins reine, ins hohe, ins torig
offene Herz träte er anders, der Gott

wirklicher Milde. Er käme gewaltig und griffe
strahlender um sich, wie Göttliche sind.
Mehr als ein Wind für die grossen gesicherten Schiffe.

Weniger nicht, als die heimliche leise Gewahrung,
die uns im Innern schweigend gewinnt
wie ein still spielendes Kind aus unendlicher Paarung.

9

*B*OAST not, you judging ones, that you dispense with torture
and that iron no longer shackles by the neck.
No heart is enhanced, not one—, because a willed
spasm of mercy more tenderly twists you.

What it received through the ages the scaffold will give
back again, as children their toys of the previous year's
birthday. Into the pure, the high, the gate-like
open heart he would differently enter, the god

of real mercy. Powerfully he would come
and more glorious in his sweep, as gods are.
More than a wind for the great assured ships.

Nor less than the secret subtle awareness
that wins us silently within
like a quietly playing child from an infinite pairing.

10

Alles Erworbne bedroht die Maschine, solange
sie sich erdreistet, im Geist, statt im Gehorchen, zu sein.
Dass nicht der herrlichen Hand schöneres Zögern
                                         mehr prange,
zu dem entschlossenern Bau schneidet sie steifer den Stein.

Nirgends bleibt sie zurück, dass wir ihr *ein* Mal entrönnen
und sie in stiller Fabrik ölend sich selber gehört.
Sie ist das Leben,—sie meint es am besten zu können,
die mit dem gleichen Entschluss ordnet und schafft und zerstört.

Aber noch ist uns das Dasein verzaubert; an hundert
Stellen ist es noch Ursprung. Ein Spielen von reinen
Kräften, die keiner berührt, der nicht kniet und bewundert.

Worte gehen noch zart am Unsäglichen aus . . .
Und die Musik, immer neu, aus den bebendsten Steinen,
baut im unbrauchbaren Raum ihr vergöttlichtes Haus.

10

*A*LL we have gained the machine threatens, so long
as it makes bold to exist in the spirit instead of obeying.
Lest the lovelier lingering of the glorious hand

longer invite us,
for the more resolute building starker it cuts the stone.

It nowhere stays behind so that we might just once escape it
and oiling in silent factory it would belong to itself.
It is life,—thinks *it* knows best,
that with equal resolve arrays, produces, destroys.

But to us existence is still enchanted; at a hundred
points it is origin still. A playing of pure
forces that no one touches who does not kneel and marvel.

Words still gently fade before the unsayable . . .
And music, ever new, out of most tremulous stones
builds in unusable space her deified house.

11

Manche, des Todes, entstand ruhig geordnete Regel,
weiterbezwingender Mensch, seit du im Jagen beharrst;
mehr doch als Falle und Netz, weiss ich dich,

Streifen von Segel,
den man hinuntergehängt in den höhligen Karst.

Leise liess man dich ein, als wärst du ein Zeichen,
Frieden zu feiern. Doch dann: rang dich am Rande der Knecht,
—und, aus den Höhlen, die Nacht warf eine Handvoll

von bleichen
taumelnden Tauben ins Licht . . .

Aber auch *das* ist im Recht.

Fern von dem Schauenden sei jeglicher Hauch des Bedauerns,
nicht *nur* vom Jäger allein, der, was sich zeitig erweist,
wachsam und handelnd vollzieht.

Töten ist eine Gestalt unseres wandernden Trauerns . . .
Rein ist im heiteren Geist,
was an uns selber geschieht.

11

MANY a calmly established rule of death has come about,
further-conquering man, since first you held to your
                                                        hunting;
yet more than of trap or net I know of you, strip of sail,
that they used to hang down into the cavernous Karst.

Softly they let you in, as though you had been a signal
to celebrate peace. But then: at the edge the boy gave you
                                                        a twist,
—and, out of the caves, the night threw a handful of pale
tumbling pigeons into the light . . .
                        But even that has its rightness.

Far from the onlooker be every breath of pity,
not from the hunter merely, who, proceeding, alert,
fulfills that which is timely.

Killing is a form of our wandering sorrow . . .
Pure in the spirit serene
is what happens to ourselves.

12

WOLLE die Wandlung. O sei für die Flamme begeistert,
drin sich ein Ding dir entzieht, das mit Verwandlungen prunkt;
jener entwerfende Geist, welcher das Irdische meistert,
liebt in dem Schwung der Figur nichts wie den
                                        wendenden Punkt.

Was sich ins Bleiben verschliesst, schon *ists* das Erstarrte;
wähnt es sich sicher im Schutz des unscheinbaren Grau's?
Warte, ein Härtestes warnt aus der Ferne das Harte.
Wehe—: abwesender Hammer holt aus!

Wer sich als Quelle ergiesst, den erkennt die Erkennung;
und sie führt ihn entzückt durch das heiter Geschaffne,
das mit Anfang oft schliesst und mit Ende beginnt.

Jeder glückliche Raum ist Kind oder Enkel von Trennung,
den sie staunend durchgehn. Und die verwandelte Daphne
will, seit sie lorbeern fühlt, dass du dich wandelst in Wind.

12

WILL transformation. O be enraptured with flame,
wherein a thing eludes you that is boastful with changes;
that projecting spirit, which masters the earthly,
loves in the swing of the figure nothing so much as the
                                         point of inflection.

What shuts itself into remaining already *is* starkness;
does it think itself safe in the shelter of inconspicuous gray?
Beware, from afar a hardest comes warning the hard.
Woe—, an absent hammer lifts!

Who pours himself forth as a spring, him Cognizance knows;
and she leads him enchanted through the realm of serene
                                         creation,
that often ends with beginning and with ending begins.

Every happy space they wander wondering through
is child or grandchild of parting. And the transformed Daphne,
                                         since feeling
laurel-like, wants you to change yourself into wind.

13

Sᴇɪ allem Abschied voran, als wäre er hinter
dir, wie der Winter, der eben geht.
Denn unter Wintern ist einer so endlos Winter,
dass, überwinternd, dein Herz überhaupt übersteht.

Sei immer tot in Eurydike—, singender steige,
preisender steige zurück in den reinen Bezug.
Hier, unter Schwindenden, sei, im Reiche der Neige,
sei ein klingendes Glas, das sich im Klang schon zerschlug.

Sei—und wisse zugleich des Nicht-Seins Bedingung,
den unendlichen Grund deiner innigen Schwingung,
dass du sie völlig vollziehst dieses einzige Mal.

Zu dem gebrauchten sowohl, wie zum dumpfen und stummen
Vorrat der vollen Natur, den unsäglichen Summen,
zähle dich jubelnd hinzu und vernichte die Zahl.

13

B E in advance of all parting, as though it were
behind you like the winter that is just going.
For among winters one is so endlessly winter
that, overwintering, your heart once for all will hold out.

Be ever dead in Eurydice—, mount more singingly,
mount more praisingly back into the pure relation.
Here, among the waning, be, in the realm of decline,
be a ringing glass that shivers even as it rings.

Be—and at the same time know the condition
of not-being, the infinite ground of your deep vibration,
that you may fully fulfill it this single time.

To the used as well as the muffled and mute
store of full Nature, the uncountable sums,
jubilant add yourself and cancel the count.

14

Siehe die Blumen, diese dem Irdischen treuen,
denen wir Schicksal vom Rande des Schicksals leihn,—
aber wer weiss es! Wenn sie ihr Welken bereuen,
ist es an uns, ihre Reue zu sein.

Alles will schweben. Da gehn wir umher wie Beschwerer,
legen auf alles uns selbst, vom Gewichte entzückt;
o was sind wir den Dingen für zehrende Lehrer,
weil ihnen ewige Kindheit glückt.

Nähme sie einer ins innige Schlafen und schliefe
tief mit den Dingen—: o wie käme er leicht,
anders zum anderen Tag, aus der gemeinsamen Tiefe.

Oder er bliebe vielleicht; und sie blühten und priesen
ihn, den Bekehrten, der nun den Ihrigen gleicht,
allen den stillen Geschwistern im Winde der Wiesen.

14

*S*ᴇᴇ the flowers, faithful to what is earthly,
to whom we lend fate from the border of fate,—
yet who knows! If they regret their wilting,
it is for us to be their regret.

All things want to float. And we go about like **weights,**
lay our self upon everything, delighted with **gravity;**
O what wearing teachers we are for things,
while they succeed at eternal childhood.

If one took them into intimate slumber and slept
deeply with things—: o how lightly he would **come,**
another to another day, out of the common deep.

Or he would **stay** perhaps; and they would bloom **and praise
him,** the convert, who is now like one of them, like **all
those** quiet sisters and brothers in the wind of **the meadows.**

15

O Brunnen-Mund, du gebender, du Mund,
der unerschöpflich Eines, Reines, spricht,—
du, vor des Wassers fliessendem Gesicht,
marmorne Maske. Und im Hintergrund

der Aquädukte Herkunft. Weither an
Gräbern vorbei, vom Hang des Apennins
tragen sie dir dein Sagen zu, das dann
am schwarzen Altern deines Kinns

vorüberfällt in das Gefäss davor.
Dies ist das schlafend hingelegte Ohr,
das Marmor-Ohr, in das du immer sprichst.

Ein Ohr der Erde. Nur mit sich allein
redet sie also. Schiebt ein Krug sich ein,
so scheint es ihr, dass du sie unterbrichst.

15

O fountain-mouth, o giving, o mouth that speaks
exhaustlessly one single, one pure thing,—
before the water's flowing face,
you marble mask. And in the background

coming of aqueducts. From far away
passing by graves, from the slope of the Appenines
they bring to you your speaking, that then falls
past the blackened aging of your chin

into the basin there before it.
This is the ear laid sleeping down,
the marble ear in which you always speak.

An ear of earth's. So that she's only talking
with herself. If a pitcher slips between,
it seems to her that you are interrupting.

16

IMMER wieder von uns aufgerissen,
ist der Gott die Stelle, welche heilt.
Wir sind Scharfe, denn wir wollen wissen,
aber er ist heiter und verteilt.

Selbst die reine, die geweihte Spende
nimmt er anders nicht in seine Welt,
als indem er sich dem freien Ende
unbewegt entgegenstellt.

Nur der Tote trinkt
aus der hier von uns *gehörten* Quelle,
wenn der Gott ihm schweigend winkt, dem Toten.

Uns wird nur das Lärmen angeboten.
Und das Lamm erbittet seine Schelle
aus dem stilleren Instinkt.

16

TORN open by us ever and again,
the god is the place that heals.
We are sharp, because we want to know,
but he is serene and diffused.

Even the pure, the consecrate libation
he takes no differently into his world
than by setting himself motionless
opposite the free end.

Only the dead drink
out of the spring here *heard* by us,
when the god signs to them silently, the dead.

To *us* only the noise is proffered.
And the lamb begs for its bell
out of more quiet instinct.

17

*W*o, in welchen immer selig bewässerten Gärten, an

welchen

Bäumen, aus welchen zärtlich entblätterten Blüten-Kelchen
reifen die fremdartigen Früchte der Tröstung? Diese
köstlichen, deren du eine vielleicht in der zertretenen Wiese

deiner Armut findest. Von einem zum anderen Male
wunderst du dich über die Grösse der Frucht,
über ihr Heilsein, über die Sanftheit der Schale,
und dass sie der Leichtsinn des Vogels dir nicht vorwegnahm
und nicht die Eifersucht

unten des Wurms. Gibt es denn Bäume, von Engeln beflogen,
und von verborgenen langsamen Gärtnern so seltsam gezogen,
dass sie uns tragen, ohne uns zu gehören?

Haben wir niemals vermocht, wir Schatten und Schemen,
durch unser voreilig reifes und wieder welkes Benehmen
jener gelassenen Sommer Gleichmut zu stören?

17

*W*HERE, in what ever-blessedly watered gardens, on what
trees, out of what tenderly unleaved blossom-calyxes
do the exotic fruits of consolation ripen? Those
delicious fruits, of which you find one perhaps
                                    in the trampled meadow

of your poverty. Time and again
you marvel over the size of the fruit,
over its soundness, over the smoothness of the rind,
and that the thoughtlessness of a bird had not snatched it
                                    from you, nor the jealousy

of the worm below. Are there then trees, frequented by angels,
and so strangely reared by slow occult gardeners
that they bear for us without belonging to us?

Have we never been able, we shadows and shades,
through our behavior, ripe too soon and withered again,
to disturb the equanimity of those calm summers?

18

TÄNZERIN: o du Verlegung
alles Vergehens in Gang: wie brachtest du's dar.
Und der Wirbel am Schluss, dieser Baum aus Bewegung,
nahm er nicht ganz in Besitz das erschwungene Jahr?

Blühte nicht, dass ihn dein Schwingen von vorhin
                                        umschwärme,
plötzlich sein Wipfel von Stille? Und über ihr,
war sie nicht Sonne, war sie nicht Sommer, die Wärme,
diese unzählige Wärme aus dir?

Aber er trug auch, er trug, dein Baum der Ekstase.
Sind sie nicht seine ruhigen Früchte: der Krug,
reifend gestreift, und die gereiftere Vase?

Und in den Bildern: ist nicht die Zeichnung geblieben,
die deiner Braue dunkler Zug
rasch an die Wandung der eigenen Wendung geschrieben?

18

D ANCER: o you transposing
of all transcience into stepping: how you presented it!
And the whirl at the close, that tree out of movement,
did it not take full possession of the hard-swung year?

Did not its crown, that your swinging of a moment ago might
                                                    swarm
around it, suddenly bloom with stillness? And above,
was it not sun, was it not summer, the warmth,
that immeasurable warmth out of you?

But it bore too, it bore, your tree of ecstasy.
Are these not its tranquil fruits: the pitcher,
streaked as it ripened, and the still riper vase?

And in the pictures: did not the drawing remain
that the dark stroke of your eyebrow
swiftly wrote on the wall of its own turning?

19

IRGENDWO wohnt das Gold in der verwöhnenden Bank,
und mit Tausenden tut es vertraulich. Doch jener
Blinde, der Bettler, ist selbst dem kupfernen Zehner
wie ein verlorener Ort, wie das staubige Eck unterm Schrank.

In den Geschäften entlang ist das Geld wie zu Hause
und verkleidet sich scheinbar in Seide, Nelken und Pelz.
Er, der Schweigende, steht in der Atempause
alles des wach oder schlafend atmenden Gelds.

O wie mag sie sich schliessen bei Nacht, diese immer
                                                    offene Hand.
Morgen holt sie das Schicksal wieder, und täglich
hält es sie hin: hell, elend, unendlich zerstörbar.

Dass doch einer, ein Schauender, endlich ihren langen Bestand
staunend begriffe und rühmte. Nur dem Aufsingenden säglich.
Nur dem Göttlichen hörbar.

19

Somewhere gold lives in the pampering bank, on
                                        intimate
terms with thousands. Yet that blindman there,
that beggar, to even a copper penny is like
a lost place, like the dusty corner under the wardrobe.

In the shops all along money acts at home
and appears dressed up in silk, carnations and furs.
He, the silent one, stands in the pause between breaths
of all that breathing money as it wakes or sleeps.

O how does it close by night, that always open hand?
Tomorrow fate will fetch it again, and daily
will hold it out, lucid, wretched, ever so destructible.

If only someone, who sees, would at last in wonder conceive
and praise its long persistence. Sayable only to the singer.
Audible only to the god.

20

ZWISCHEN den Sternen, wie weit; und doch, um wievieles
                                        noch weiter,
was man am Hiesigen lernt.
Einer, zum Beispiel, ein Kind . . . und ein Nächster,
                                        ein Zweiter—,
o wie unfasslich entfernt.

Schicksal, es misst uns vielleicht mit des Seienden Spanne,
dass es uns fremd erscheint;
denk, wieviel Spannen allein vom Mädchen zum Manne,
wenn es ihn meidet und meint.

Alles ist weit—, und nirgends schliesst sich der Kreis.
Sieh in der Schüssel, auf heiter bereitetem Tische,
seltsam der Fische Gesicht.

Fische sind stumm . . . , meinte man einmal. Wer weiss?
Aber ist nicht am Ende ein Ort, wo man das, was der Fische
Sprache wäre, *ohne* sie spricht?

20

Between the stars, how far; and yet, by how much
                                                    still farther,
what we learn from the here and now.
Someone, a child, for example . . . and one next him,
                                        a second—,
o how incredibly distant.

Fate, it measures us perhaps with being's span,
that it seems strange to us;
think, how many spans merely from a maid to a man,
when she avoids him and has him in mind.

Everything is far—, and nowhere does the circle close.
See in the dish, on a gaily laid table,
how odd the faces of fishes.

Fishes are dumb . . . , one used to think. Who knows?
But is there not perhaps a place, where what would be the
                                                    fishes'
language is spoken *without* them?

21

S INGE die Gärten, mein Herz, die du nicht kennst;
                                                 wie in Glas
eingegossene Gärten, klar, unerreichbar.
Wasser und Rosen von Ispahan oder Schiras,
singe sie selig, preise sie, keinem vergleichbar.

Zeige, mein Herz, dass du sie niemals entbehrst.
Dass sie dich meinen, ihre reifenden Feigen.
Dass du mit ihren, zwischen den blühenden Zweigen
wie zum Gesicht gesteigerten Lüften verkehrst.

Meide den Irrtum, dass es Entbehrungen gebe
für den geschehnen Entschluss, diesen: zu sein!
Seidener Faden, kamst du hinein ins Gewebe.

Welchem der Bilder du auch im Innern geeint bist
(sei es selbst ein Moment aus dem Leben der Pein),
fühl, dass der ganze, der rühmliche Teppich gemeint ist.

21

S ING the gardens, my heart, that you do not know; like
                                        gardens
poured in glass, clear, unattainable.
Waters and roses of Ispahan or of Shiraz,
blissfully sing them, praise them, comparable to none.

Show, my heart, that you never miss them. That it **is**
you they have in mind, their ripening figs.
That you consort with their airs that are heightened
as though to vision between the blossoming branches.

Avoid the error of thinking something is missed
for the resolve once taken, this: to be!
Silken thread, you became part of the weaving.

Whichever the picture you are innerly one with
(be it even a moment out of the life of pain),
feel that the whole, the glorious carpet is meant.

22

O trotz Schicksal: die herrlichen Überflüsse
unseres Daseins, in Parken übergeschäumt,—
oder als steinerne Männer neben die Schlüsse
hoher Portale, unter Balkone gebäumt!

O die eherne Glocke, die ihre Keule
täglich wider den stumpfen Alltag hebt.
Oder die *eine,* in Karnak, die Säule, die Säule,
die fast ewige Tempel überlebt.

Heute stürzen die Überschüsse, dieselben,
nur noch als Eile vorbei, aus dem wagrechten gelben
Tag in die blendend mit Licht übertriebene Nacht.

Aber das Rasen zergeht und lässt keine Spuren.
Kurven des Flugs durch die Luft und die, die sie fuhren,
keine vielleicht ist umsonst. Doch nur wie gedacht.

22

O despite fate: the glorious overflowings
of our existence, foamed over into parks,—
or as men of stone beside the bases
of high portals, braced under balconies!

O the brazen bell that daily lifts
its bludgeon against the dull quotidian.
Or the *one*, in Karnak, the column, the column
that outlives almost eternal temples.

Today the abundances plunge past, the same ones,
but only as haste, out of the horizontal yellow
day into the dazzlingly magnified night.

But the frenzy passes and leaves no traces.
Curves of flight through the air, and those that led them,
none perhaps is in vain. Yet only as thought.

23

Rufe mich zu jener deiner Stunden,
die dir unaufhörlich widersteht:
flehend nah wie das Gesicht von Hunden,
aber immer wieder weggedreht,

wenn du meinst, sie endlich zu erfassen.
So Entzognes ist am meisten dein.
Wir sind frei. Wir wurden dort entlassen,
wo wir meinten, erst begrüsst zu sein.

Bang verlangen wir nach einem Halte,
wir zu Jungen manchmal für das Alte
und zu alt für das, was niemals war.

Wir, gerecht nur, wo wir dennoch preisen,
weil wir, ach, der Ast sind und das Eisen
und das Süsse reifender Gefahr.

23

Summon me to the one among your hours
that unceasingly resists you:
imploringly near as a dog's face,
but ever and again turning away

when you think at last you're grasping it.
What is thus withdrawn is most yours.
We are free. We were there dismissed
where we thought ourselves to have been welcomed.

Anxiously we clamor for a hold,
we, too young sometimes for what is old
and too old for that which never was.

We, only just where nevertheless we praise,
for we are, alas, the bough and the blade
and the sweet of ripening danger.

24

O diese Lust, immer neu, aus gelockertem Lehm!
Niemand beinah hat den frühesten Wagern geholfen.
Städte entstanden trotzdem an beseligten Golfen,
Wasser und Öl füllten die Krüge trotzdem.

Götter, wir planen sie erst in erkühnten Entwürfen,
die uns das mürrische Schicksal wieder zerstört.
Aber sie sind die Unsterblichen. Sehet, wir dürfen
jenen erhorchen, der uns am Ende erhört.

Wir, ein Geschlecht durch Jahrtausende: Mütter und Väter,
immer erfüllter von dem künftigen Kind,
dass es uns einst, übersteigend, erschüttere, später.

Wir, wir unendlich Gewagten, was haben wir Zeit!
Und nur der schweigsame Tod, der weiss, was wir sind
und was er immer gewinnt, wenn er uns leiht.

24

O this delight, ever new, out of loosened clay!
Almost nobody helped the earliest darers.
Cities arose nonetheless on blissful gulfs,
water and oil filled the pitchers nonetheless.

Gods,—we project them first in emboldened sketches
which crabbed fate destroys for us again.
But they are the immortals. Behold, we may
hearken him out who will in the end hear us.

We, a generation through thousands of years: mothers
and fathers, more and more full of the future child,
so that someday, surpassing, it may overwhelm us, later.

We, so endlessly ventured, how much time we have!
And only taciturn death, he knows what we are
and what he always gains when he lends us.

25

Schon, horch, hörst du der ersten Harken
Arbeit; wieder den menschlichen Takt
in der verhaltenen Stille der starken
Vorfrühlingserde. Unabgeschmackt

scheint dir das Kommende. Jenes so oft
dir schon Gekommene scheint dir zu kommen
wieder wie Neues. Immer erhofft,
nahmst du es niemals. Es hat dich genommen.

Selbst die Blätter durchwinterter Eichen
scheinen im Abend ein künftiges Braun.
Manchmal geben sich Lüfte ein Zeichen.

Schwarz sind die Sträucher. Doch Haufen von Dünger
lagern als satteres Schwarz in den Au'n.
Jede Stunde, die hingeht, wird jünger.

25

*H*ARK, already you can hear the working
of the first harrows; again the human rhythm
in the retentive stillness of the strong
early-spring earth. What's coming seems

not stale to you. That which already
has come to you so often seems to be coming
like something new. Always expected,
you never took it. It took you.

Even the leaves of wintered oaks
seem in the evening a future brown.
Sometimes breezes give each other a sign.

The bushes are black. Yet piles of manure
lie heaped a richer black in the fields.
Every hour that passes grows younger.

26

Wie ergreift uns der Vogelschrei . . .
Irgendein einmal erschaffenes Schreien.
Aber die Kinder schon, spielend im Freien,
schreien an wirklichen Schreien vorbei.

Schreien den Zufall. In Zwischenräume
dieses, des Weltraums, (in welchen der heile
Vogelschrei eingeht, wie Menschen in Träume—)
treiben sie ihre, des Kreischens, Keile.

Wehe, wo sind wir? Immer noch freier,
wie die losgerissenen Drachen
jagen wir halbhoch, mit Rändern von Lachen,

windig zerfetzten.— Ordne die Schreier,
singender Gott! dass sie rauschend erwachen,
tragend als Strömung das Haupt und die Leier.

26

How the cry of a bird can stir us . . .
Any once created crying.
But even children, at play in the open,
cry past real cries.

Cry chance. Into interstices
of this world-space, (into which the unbroken
bird-cry passes, as people do into dreams—)
they drive their wedges, wedges of shrieking.

O woe, where are we? More and more free,
like kites torn loose
we chase in mid-air, with edges of laughter,

windily tattered.—Array the criers,
singing god! that they waken resounding,
a current bearing the head and the lyre.

27

Gɪʙт es wirklich die Zeit, die zerstörende?
Wann, auf dem ruhenden Berg, zerbricht sie die Burg?
Dieses Herz, das unendlich den Göttern gehörende,
wann vergewaltigts der Demiurg?

Sind wir wirklich so ängstlich Zerbrechliche,
wie das Schicksal uns wahrmachen will?
Ist die Kindheit, die tiefe, versprechliche,
in den Wurzeln—später—still?

Ach, das Gespenst des Vergänglichen,
durch den arglos Empfänglichen
geht es, als wär es ein Rauch.

Als die, die wir sind, als die Treibenden,
gelten wir doch bei bleibenden
Kräften als göttlicher Brauch.

27

Does it really exist, time the destroyer?
When, on the mountain at rest, will it crumble the castle?
This heart, that belongs to the gods unendingly,
when will the demiurge overcome it by force?

Are we really so apprehensively fragile
as fate would have us believe?
Is childhood, so deep, so promiseful,
at the roots of it—later—stilled?

Ah, the specter of transience,
through the simply receptive
it passes as though it were smoke.

As those that we are, with our driving,
we yet count among abiding
powers as a use of the gods.

28

O komm und geh. Du, fast noch Kind, ergänze
für einen Augenblick die Tanzfigur
zum reinen Sternbild eines jener Tänze,
darin wir die dumpf ordnende Natur

vergänglich übertreffen. Denn sie regte
sich völlig hörend nur, da Orpheus sang.
Du warst noch die von damals her Bewegte
und leicht befremdet, wenn ein Baum sich lang

besann, mit dir nach dem Gehör zu gehn.
Du wusstest noch die Stelle, wo die Leier
sich tönend hob—; die unerhörte Mitte.

Für sie versuchtest du die schönen Schritte
und hofftest, einmal zu der heilen Feier
des Freundes Gang und Antlitz hinzudrehn.

28

O come and go. You, still half a child,
fill out the dance-figure for a moment
to the pure constellation of one of those
dances in which we fleetingly transcend

dumbly ordering Nature. For she roused
to full hearing only when Orpheus sang.
You were the one still moved from that earlier time
and a little surprised if a tree took long to consider

whether to go along with you by ear.
You still knew the place where the lyre
lifted sounding—: the unheard-of center.

For this you tried the lovely steps and hoped
one day towards the perfect celebration
to turn the pace and countenance of your friend.

29

Stiller Freund der vielen Fernen, fühle,
wie dein Atem noch den Raum vermehrt.
Im Gebälk der finstern Glockenstühle
lass dich läuten. Das, was an dir zehrt,

wird ein Starkes über dieser Nahrung.
Geh in der Verwandlung aus und ein.
Was ist deine leidendste Erfahrung?
Ist dir Trinken bitter, werde Wein.

Sei in dieser Nacht aus Übermass
Zauberkraft am Kreuzweg deiner Sinne,
ihrer seltsamen Begegnung Sinn.

Und wenn dich das Irdische vergass,
zu der stillen Erde sag: Ich rinne.
Zu dem raschen Wasser sprich: Ich bin.

29

SILENT friend of many distances,
feel how your breath is still increasing space.
Among the beams of the dark belfries let
yourself ring out. What feeds on you

will grow strong upon this nourishment.
Be conversant with transformation.
From what experience have you suffered most?
Is drinking bitter to you, turn to wine.

Be, in this immeasurable night,
magic power at your senses' crossroad,
be the meaning of their strange encounter.

And if the earthly has forgotten you,
say to the still earth: I flow.
To the rapid water speak: I am.

Notes

Rilke was born in Prague on December 4, 1875, and died at Val-Mont, near Glion, Switzerland, on December 29, 1926.

Unless otherwise stated, the letter-passages quoted are taken from the Insel-Verlag's six-volume edition of the *Letters* (*Briefe*) and the additional volume of *Letters to His Publisher* (*Briefe an seinen Verleger*, 1934). *G.W.* refers to the six-volume edition of the *Collected Works* (*Gesammelte Werke*, 1930), and *A.W.* to the two-volume *Selected Works* (*Ausgewählte Werke*, 1938).

*   *   *   *

A year after the completion of the *Sonnets*, Rilke wrote (to Xaver von Moos, April 20, 1923):

Even I am just beginning to penetrate more and more into the spirit of this sending, for such the Sonnets appear to be. As for their comprehensibility, I am now fully able to impart these poems accurately in reading them aloud. . . . I was extremely absorbed and gratified recently in testing this out.

And he adds (to his wife, April 23) that

with little aids I am able to slip in as I read them . . . the continuity becomes everywhere apparent, and where some obscurity remains it is of the sort that demands not clearing-up (*Aufklärung*) but subjection (*Unterwerfung*).

Of the *Sonnets* and the *Duino Elegies,* which had been completed at Muzot during the same period, he writes a Swiss friend (December 22, 1923):

In you, dear Nanny von Escher, such ancient and unalloyed qualities of this varied land come together, that I feel a sort of satisfaction in showing you in these books what I have achieved upon its honest soil and under its protection. Much —about this I do not deceive myself—in the course and continuity of these verses you will find difficult of approach. . . . But it lies in the nature of these poems, in their condensation and abbreviation (in the way they often state lyric totals instead of lining up the stages necessary to the result), that they seem intended to be generally grasped rather through inspiration in those similarly directed than with what is called 'understanding'. Two inmost experiences were decisive for their production: the determination constantly maturing in me to keep life open towards death, and, on the other hand, the intellectual necessity of instating the transformations of love differently in this wider whole than was possible in the narrower orbit of life (which simply excluded death as the Other). It is here that one should, so to say, seek the 'plot' of these poems, and now and then it stands, I believe, simple and strong in the foreground.

Two years later (March 11, 1925) he expressed to his publisher a wish to have a copy of the *Sonnets*—of the *Elegies,* too, but "quite particularly of the Sonnets"—so interleaved with blank pages that he could, when the spirit moved him, add in some short commentaries to the more difficult poems. He never carried out this plan; but it may have arisen in his mind some months earlier in connection with a questionnaire from his Polish translator, Witold von Hulewicz, to which he had replied at some length (November 13, 1925). That part of the reply which concerns the *Sonnets* and the *Elegies* is perhaps the fullest statement Rilke ever committed to paper outside of the works themselves, and, though not new to some readers—Mr. J. B. Leishman draws upon it in the interesting discussion to be found in the notes to his version of the *Sonnets* (London, Hogarth Press, 1936)—it is worth quoting in full here for its exposition of what Rilke means by "keeping life open towards death" and "the transformations of love":

And is it *I* who may give the Elegies their right explanation? They reach out infinitely beyond me. I hold them for a further shaping of those essential assumptions already given in the 'Stundenbuch', that in the two parts of the 'Neue Gedichte' play with the picture of the world experimentally and then in Malte, drawn together at cross purposes, strike back into life and there almost lead to the conclusion that this life thus suspended in the groundless is impossible. In the 'Elegies', from the same premises, life becomes possible again, indeed it here comes to know that final *affirmation* to which young Malte, though on the difficult right road 'des longues études', was not yet able to lead it. *Affirmation of life* AND *death appears as one in the 'Ele-*

gies'. To admit the one without the other is, as is here learned and celebrated, a limitation that in the end excludes all infinity. Death is the *side of life* that is turned away from us: we must try to achieve the fullest consciousness of our existence, which is at home in *the two unseparated realms, inexhaustibly nourished by both*. . . . The true figure of life extends through *both* domains, the blood of the mightiest circulation drives through *both: there is neither a here nor a beyond, but the great unity,* in which those creatures that surpass us, the 'angels', are at home. And now the place of the love-problem in this world broadened by the larger half of itself, in this world only now *complete,* only now *whole.* It astonishes me that the 'Sonnets to Orpheus', which are at least as 'difficult', filled with the same essence, are not more helpful to your understanding of the 'Elegies'. These latter were begun in 1912 (at Duino), continued—fragmentarily—in Spain and Paris till 1914; the war completely interrupted this my biggest work; when I dared take it up again (here) in 1922, the new Elegies and their termination were preceded by the 'Sonnets to Orpheus', which stormily imposed themselves (they were *not* in my plan). They are, as could not be otherwise, of the same 'birth' as the 'Elegies', and their sudden coming up, without my willing it, in association with a girl who died young, moves them still nearer to the well-spring of their origin; this association is one more connection towards the center of *that* realm the depth and influence of which we, everywhere unboundaried, share with the dead and with those to come. We, of this earth and this today, are not for a moment hedged by the world of time, nor bound within it: we are incessantly flowing over and over to those who preceded us and to those who ap-

parently come after us. In that widest *'open'* world all *are,*
one cannot say 'simultaneously', for the very falling away
of time conditions their *existing.* Transience everywhere
plunges into a deep being. And so all forms of this earth are
not only not to be used in a time-limited way only, but, so
far as we are able, to be given place in those superior sig-
nificances in which we have a part. *Not,* however, *in the
Christian sense* (from which I more and more passionately
depart); but, in an earthly, a deeply earthly, a blissfully
earthly consciousness we must introduce what is *here* seen
and touched into that wider, that widest circuit. Not into
a beyond the shadow of which darkens the earth, but into
a whole, *into the whole.* Nature, the things we move among
and use, are provisional and perishable; but, so long as we
are here, they are *our* possession and our friendship, sharing
the knowledge of our grief and gladness, as they have al-
ready been the confidants of our forebears. Hence it is im-
portant not only not to run down and degrade everything
earthly, but just because of its temporariness, which it shares
with us, we ought to grasp and transform these phenomena
and these things in a most loving understanding. Trans-
form? Yes; for our task is so deeply and so passionately to
impress upon ourselves this provisional and perishable earth,
that its essential being will arise again 'invisibly' in us. *We
are the bees of the invisible. We frantically plunder the
visible of its honey, to accumulate it in the great golden hive
of the invisible.* The 'Elegies' show us at this work, the work
of these continual conversions of the beloved visible and
tangible into the invisible vibration and animation of our
[own] nature, which introduces new frequencies into the
vibration-spheres of the universe. (Since the various ele-

ments in the cosmos are merely different rates of vibration,
we are preparing in this way not only new intensities of a
spiritual sort but, who knows, new substances, metals, neb-
ulae and stars.) And this activity is singularly supported
and urged on through the ever more rapid disappearance
of so much of the visible that is not going to be replaced.
To our grandparents a 'house', a 'well', a tower familiar to
them, even their own dress, their cloak, was still infinitely
more, infinitely more intimate: almost each thing a vessel
in which they found something human and into which they
set aside something human. Now, from America, empty
indifferent things are crowding over to us, sham things,
life-decoys. . . . A house, in the American understanding,
an American apple or a grapevine there, has *nothing* in
common with the house, the fruit, the grape, into which
went the hopes and meditations of our forefathers. . . .
Animated things, things experienced by us, *and that know
us,* are on the decline and cannot be replaced any more.
We are perhaps the last still to have known such things.
On us rests the responsibility of upholding not only the
memory of *them* (that would be little and unreliable), but
their human and laral worth. ('Laral' in the sense of house-
hold gods.) The earth has no other way out than to become
invisible: *in* us, who with a part of our being participate in
the invisible, have (at least) certificates of participation in
it, and can increase our holdings in invisibility during our
being-here,—*in* us alone can be fulfilled this intimate and
continual transformation of the visible into invisibility that
is no longer dependent on the being visible and tangible, just
as our own destiny continually grows *simultaneously more
present and invisible* in us. The Elegies set up this norm

of existence: they affirm, they celebrate this consciousness. They carefully range it among its traditions, calling upon age-old transmissions and rumors of transmissions to support this conjecture and even invoking in the Egyptian cult of the dead a foreknowledge of such relationships. (Although the 'Lament-land' through which the elder 'Lament' leads the dead youth is *not* to be *identified* with Egypt, but is only, in a way, a reflection of the Nile country in the desert-clarity of the consciousness of the dead.) If one makes the mistake of holding up Catholic conceptions of death, of the beyond and of eternity, to the Elegies or Sonnets, one is getting entirely away from their point of departure and preparing for oneself a more and more thorough misunderstanding. The 'angel' of the Elegies has nothing to do with the angel of the Christian heaven (more nearly with the angelic figures of Islam) . . . The angel of the *Elegies* is that creature in which the transformation of the visible into invisibility, which we are accomplishing, appears already fulfilled. For the angel of the Elegies all past towers and palaces are extant because long since invisible, and the still standing towers and bridges of our existence, *already* invisible, although (for us) they still physically continue. The angel of the Elegies is that being which stands security for recognizing in the invisible a higher level of reality.—Therefore 'terrible' to us because we, its lovers and transformers, are still clinging to the visible.—All the worlds of the universe fling themselves into the invisible as into their next-deeper reality; *some stars heighten directly in intensity and pass away in the infinite consciousness of the angels—, others are dependent on creatures who slowly and laboriously transform them, in whose terror and ecstasy they*

reach their next invisible realization. We are, be it empha-
sized once more, *in the sense of the Elegies we are these
transformers of the earth; our whole existence, the flights
and downfalls of our love, all capacitate us for this task* (be-
side which, essentially, no other holds). (The Sonnets show
details from this activity, which here appears placed under
the name and protection of a dead girl whose incompletion
and innocence holds open the door of the grave, so that she,
gone from us, belongs to those powers who keep half of life
fresh and open towards the other wound-open half.) Ele-
gies and Sonnets continually bear each other out—, and I
see an infinite grace in my having been allowed to fill both
these sails with one breath: the little rust-colored sail of the
Sonnets and the gigantic white canvas of the Elegies.

May you, dear friend, find some advice and some elucida-
tion here and, for the rest, continue to help yourself. For:
I do not know whether I would ever be able to say more.

* * * *

Foreword

The opening quotation is from Rilke's letter to Xaver von Moos of April 20, 1923.

The two quotations in the second paragraph come, respectively, from the letter to his publisher of February 23, 1922, and that to Inga Junghans of April 5, 1923.

The same letter to his publisher attests to the part played by the death of Vera Knoop, while the engraving of Orpheus is described by his publisher's wife, Frau Katharina Kippenberg, in her *Rainer Maria Rilke, Ein Beitrag* (1935).

Rilke's comments on the possible difficulties of the *Sonnets* are taken from the above-mentioned letter to Xaver von Moos and that to Leopold von Schloezer of March 23, 1923.

The passage quoted in the penultimate paragraph is from a letter of June 1, 1923, to the Countess Sizzo, in the Rilke Archive at Weimar. For this, as for some other items, I am indebted to the excellent article of Mr. Dieter Bassermann, "Engel und Orpheus," in *Die Neue Rundschau,* April, 1939.

First Part

Sonnet 1

When Orpheus, singing, sought his dead Eurydice, according
to Virgil "the very halls of hell were spell-bound", and according
to Ovid "the bloodless spirits wept"; and when he mourned her
once more lost, the power of his song is described by Virgil as
"charming the tigers, and making the oaks attend his strain",
while Ovid names the many kinds of trees that came to make a
shade about the grassy hill where he "sat down and smote his
sounding lyre". Again the influence that fascinates and soothes
makes its appeal to the Elizabethan imagination:

> Orpheus with his lute made trees
> And the mountain tops that freeze
> Bow themselves when he did sing:
> To his music plants and flowers
> Ever sprung; as sun and showers
>   There had made a lasting spring.
>
> Every thing that heard him play,
> Even the billows of the sea,
> Hung their heads and then lay by.
> In sweet music is such art,
>   Killing care and grief of heart
>   Fall asleep, or hearing, die.

The song of Rilke's Orpheus, of which the tall tree itself becomes a symbol, seems to waken a wider awareness in them as it "teaches the creatures their ear".

Sonnet 2

Sometimes it is to Orpheus, sometimes to the poet in general that the *Sonnets* are addressed; sometimes they concern Rilke himself. While he does not say that this poem refers to her, it seems to be one of the sonnets that "hover about the relationship" with Vera Knoop.

Vera, who was born in Moscow, October 15, 1900, and was barely twenty when she died, seems to have been extraordinarily gifted in the arts, especially music and dancing. Rilke described her (to Countess Sizzo) as

> that beautiful child, who had just begun to dance and attracted the attention of everyone who saw her in those days through the art of motion and transformation innate in her body and spirit.

Elsewhere he speaks of having known Vera's father, Gerhard Ouckama Knoop, a chemist, poet, and novelist, not particularly well,

> but there existed between us from the first that instinctive confidence, that joy in each other that needs no further proof—which perhaps sprang from the same source as the extraordinary inspiration that has now so incredibly endowed me in setting up this monument to young Vera.

(For the foregoing I am indebted to Frau Gertrude Ouckama Knoop herself, who kindly wrote down a few notes at the request of mutual friends.)

After reading her account of Vera's illness and death, he wrote Frau Knoop (presumably on the evening of New Year's Day, 1922):

Were one to read this about any young girl one had not known, it would touch one nearly enough. And now it concerns Vera, whose dark, singularly composed charm is to me so utterly unforgettable and so incredibly recallable that at the very moment of writing this I would fear to close my eyes lest I suddenly feel myself, here, in my present consciousness, completely overwhelmed by it.

How much, how very, very much she *was* all that, *that* to which these recollections of your suffering bear such deep irrevocable witness,—and, isn't it so? how wonderful, how unique, how incomparable a human being is! There now arose, when everything was allowed to use itself up suddenly which otherwise might have lasted for a long being-here (where?),—there now arose this excess of light in the girl's heart, and in it appear so infinitely illumined the two extreme borders of her pure insight: *this,* that pain is a mistake, a mute misunderstanding, bodily in origin, that drives its wedge, its stony wedge, into the unity of heaven and earth—, and on the other side this harmonious being-one of her heart, opened to everything, *with* this unity of the existing and continuing world, this acceptance of life, this joyful, this much-moved, this to ultimate capacity belonging way into the here and now—alas, only into the here and now?! No, (which she could not know in those first attacks of breakup and farewell!)—into the *whole,* into a far more than here and now. Oh, how, how she loved, how she reached with her heart's antennae out beyond everything here graspable and embraceable—, in those sweet hovering pauses in pain, that, full of the dream of recovery, were still granted her. . . .

Sonnet 5

In a letter to Frau Nanny Wunderly-Volkart (postmarked July 29, 1920; J. R. von Salis, *Rainer Maria Rilkes Schweizer Jahre,* 1938, p. 138) Rilke wrote:

The poet, where it is no longer a matter of a great name . . . it is all the same, it is the poet, for in the final sense there is but one, that infinite one, making himself felt here and there through the ages in some mind that is subject to him.

And in the early play *Das tägliche Leben* occurs the line (Eudo Mason, *Lebenshaltung und Symbolik bei Rainer Maria Rilke,* 1939, p. 187):

—often my favorite poems seem to me to be all by one poet.

Sonnet 6

The willow, among its many uses for mankind, has long served as an emblem of sorrow. Frazer finds (*The Golden Bough,* 3rd edition, II, 294) some reason to suppose

that when Orpheus in like manner (to Aeneas whom Virgil has descending to the subterranean world with the Golden

Bough) descended alive to hell to rescue the soul of his dead
wife Eurydice from the shades, he carried with him a willow
bough to serve as a passport on his journey to and from the
land of the dead; for in the great frescoes representing the
nether world, with which the master hand of Polygnotus
adorned the walls of a loggia at Delphi, Orpheus was de-
picted sitting pensively under a willow, holding his lyre,
now silent and useless in his left hand, while with his right
he grasped the drooping boughs of the tree.

Sonnet 7

Shelley's *Orpheus* (1820) says of the poet's song:

> . . . Unlike all human works,
> It never slackens, and through every change
> Wisdom and beauty and the power divine
> Of mighty poesy together dwell,
> Mingling in sweet accord . . .

Although Rilke had written of the First Part of the *Sonnets*
that "not a word was doubtful or needed alteration", his better
judgment did shortly cause him to substitute the present poem
for a first version which, with exception of the first stanza which
remains the same, he says "always distressed me by its pathos
and which I have long since crossed out" (to Frau Knoop,
March 18, 1922).

earthsmoke: the herb, fumitory (Fumaria officinalis).

finger-ring, clasp and jug: objects worn or used by the living,
buried with the dead.

Sonnet 8

Rilke had written in 1912 (to N. N., November 17, from Toledo):

> one may only use the strings of lament to the full if one is determined later to play, upon them, with their means, the whole jubilance that grows and gathers behind everything burdensome, painful and endured, and without which the voices are not complete.

Sonnet 10

In the first stanza Rilke has in mind the Roman sarcophagi, used as troughs, into which had been turned "eternal water from the ancient aqueducts" (—he had spent the winter of 1903–4 in Rome); in the second, as he himself indicates in one of the notes he made in the copy of the *Sonnets* presented to his friends the Leopold von Schloezers,

> 'or those': those other uncovered sarcophagi in the famous cemetery of 'Aliscamps' (near Arles), out of which flowers bloom.

That these stone coffins had long been of significance for him is evident from the closing pages of Malte's notebooks (*Die Aufzeichnungen des Malte Laurids Brigge,* 1910, published in this country as *The Journal of My Other Self,* 1930), where he asks if he should see the Prodigal Son

> in the spirit-haunted shade of Aliscamps as, among graves that stand open like the graves of those who have risen from the dead, his eyes pursue a dragon-fly?

They also appear in the poem "Römische Sarkophage" in the first part (1903–1907) of *Neue Gedichte* (*G.W.*, III, 50), in which Rilke speaks of the slow dissolution of the body in the sarcophagus,

> till it was swallowed by the unknown mouths
> that never talk. (Where does there exist and think
> a brain that someday might make use of them?)

In Munich, in 1915, he had met Alfred Schuler and felt himself (as he wrote the Princess Marie von Thurn und Taxis-Hohenlohe on March 18) both "attracted to and divided from" the arguments advanced in a lecture by "that singular solitary", who

> from an intuitive understanding of old imperial Rome undertook to give an explanation of the world which presented the dead as the actually being, the realm of the dead as a single incredible existence, but our little life's-respite as a sort of exemption from it . . .

although on Schuler's death, eight years later, he remarked to his wife (April 23, 1923) that

> in the Sonnets to Orpheus there is much that even Schuler would have admitted; indeed, who knows whether the expressing of so much of it openly and at the same time mysteriously does not derive from the contact with him.

(Some of Schuler's poems and lecture-material have been published in *Alfred Schuler, Fragmente und Vorträge aus dem Nachlass,* Johann Ambrosius Barth-Verlag, Leipzig, 1940.)

The last two lines of this sonnet give rise to much discussion. It is evident that they may also be translated:

> The lingering hour molds these two
> in the countenance of man.

Sonnet 11

Mizar, the middle star in the handle of the Great Dipper or Bear (Zeta Ursae Majoris, itself one of the most beautiful and perhaps the best known of the telescopic double stars), and the little star Alcor, that lies above and to the naked eye forms a double with it, were known to the Arabs as "The Horse and the Rider". In the Tenth Elegy, Rilke also names the Rider among "the stars of the land of pain".

Sonnets 13 and 15

A passage from the prose-fragment of 1919 entitled "Primeval Sound" (*Ur-Geräusch, G.W.,* IV, 285; *A.W.,* II, 274)—in which Rilke speculates upon what sort of music might be produced if the coronal suture of the human skull could be treated like the sound-track of a phonograph record—may be of interest in connection with the quality characteristic of these two poems:

> At a certain time, when I began to busy myself with Arabic poems, in the creation of which the five senses seemed to take part more immediately and more uniformly, it first struck me how unevenly and separately the present-day European poet uses these conductors, of which practically but one, that of sight, overladen with world, constantly over-

powers him; how trifling in comparison is even the contribu-
tion that flows in through his inattentive hearing, not to
speak of the indifference of the remaining senses, that busy
themselves only apart and with many interruptions in their
use-limited domains. And yet the perfect poem can come
into being only under the condition that the world, grasped
by five levers at once, appear under a particular aspect upon
that supernatural plane which is the plane of the poem itself.
. . . If one depicts the world's entire realm of experience,
including the regions that are beyond us, in a full circle,
it at once becomes apparent how much greater are the black
sectors indicating that which we cannot experience, com-
pared to the uneven light sectors that correspond to the
searchlights of sensuality. . . . The poet . . . must contin-
ually use the sense-sectors according to their breadth, and so
too he must wish to spread each separate one as wide as pos-
sible. . . . The question arises here whether the work of
the investigator can materially broaden the spread of these
sectors in the plane assumed by us? Whether the achieve-
ments of the microscope, the telescope and so many devices
for shifting the senses up or down, do not take their places
in *another* layer, since most of the increase thus won can not
be penetrated by the senses, hence not really 'experienced'.
It may not be premature to suppose that the artist, who de-
velops this (if one may call it so) five-fingered hand of his
senses to an ever more lively and intellectual grip, is the one
who is working most definitely at a widening of the individ-
ual sense-fields, only that his proof-bearing achievement,
since it is in the last analysis impossible without a miracle,
does not permit him to enter upon the open universal map
his personal gain in territory.

Sonnet 16

Writing of it to his wife (April 23, 1923) Rilke admits that this poem

one has to know—or guess—is addressed to a dog; I did not want to make a note, just because I wanted to take him completely into the whole. Any indication would only have isolated him again, singled him out. (This way he takes part down below, belonging and warned, like the dog and the child in Rembrandt's Night Watch.)

Dogs had a special significance for Rilke. His description, in the prose-fragment "A Meeting" (*Eine Begegnung, G.W.,* IV, 233; *A.W.,* II, 251), of a dog that attached itself to him on a walk is that of an understanding observer; the poem "Der Hund" (*Neue Gedichte,* 1908, *G.W.,* III, 253) shows equally understanding observation of the dog dealing with the fragments of our world that come to him. Near the close of Malte's notebooks (*G.W.,* V, 291; *A.W.,* II, 206), the Prodigal Son

could not have put it into words, but when he roamed out of doors all day and did not even want to have the dogs with him, it was because they too loved him; because he could read in their eyes observation and complicity, expectation and solicitude; because even in their presence he could do nothing without pleasing or hurting. . . .

While staying at Duino in 1912, he declined (to N. N., February 8) to look after a friend's dog because

where dogs are concerned it is quite particularly hard for me not to sacrifice myself: they go so utterly to my heart, these creatures who are entirely dependent upon us, whom we have helped up to a soul for which there is no heaven. Though I need my heart intact, it would probably end, tragically end, with my breaking off little morsels from the edge of it at first, then ever larger pieces towards the middle (as dogbiscuit) for this Pierrot, crying for you, no longer understanding life; I would after a little hesitation give up my profession and live entirely for his consolation. . . .

At Muzot also he refused the companionship of a dog (December 29, 1921) lest this

result in much too much relationship . . . everything alive, that makes *demands,* hits upon an infinite desire in me to admit that it is right, from the consequences of which I must then painfully disengage myself again when I realize that they are using me up completely.

Lou Andreas-Salomé (in her *Rainer Maria Rilke,* 1929, p. 68) quotes him as writing of an experience which occurred in December, 1911:

. . . once when in Kairouan, south of Tunis, a yellow Kabyle dog jumped at me and bit me (the first time in my life, in which the behavior of dogs was not without relationship), I decided that he was right, he was only expressing in his own way that I was in the wrong, with everything.

Small wonder, then, that in replying (February 26, 1924) to an inquiry about "influences," he should have headed a list of those experiences, "in themselves unemphatic," which were perhaps most important for his development, with mention of "association with a dog."

Rilke's note:

penultimate line: through 'my master's hand' the relationship to Orpheus is reëstablished, who counts here as the poet's 'master'.

Elsewhere in this connection he adds (to Countess Sizzo, June 1, 1923, Rilke Archive):

The poet wants to guide this hand so that it may for its infinite sympathy's and devotion's sake bless the dog, who, almost like Esau, has put on his pelt simply in order to share in his heart with joy and sorrow in a heritage of everything human that was not coming to him.

Sonnet 20

Immediately upon the completion of the *Duino Elegies,* on the evening of February 11, 1922, Rilke wrote to Lou Andreas-Salomé:

And imagine, *one thing* more, in another connection . . . I wrote, *made,* the horse, you know, the free happy white horse with the hobble on his foot, who once towards evening on a Volga meadow came bounding in our direction at a gallop—:

how

I did make him as an 'ex-voto' for Orpheus!—What is time? —When is present? Across so many years he sprang, with his complete happiness, into my wide-open feeling.

And later to his wife (April 23, 1923):

> Isn't it lovely that the white horse . . . I 'experienced'
> with Lou on a meadow in Russia in 1899 or 1900, bounded
> through my heart again?! That after all nothing is lost!

Sonnet 21

Rilke had written Vera's mother (February 7, 1922):

> Should the Sonnets to Orpheus ever reach publication, two
> or three of them, which, I have already noticed, presumably
> just served as conduits for the stream (as for example the
> XXIst) and remained empty after it had gone through,
> would probably have to be replaced by others.

Two days later he followed this with:

> It makes me so uncomfortable to think of that XXIst poem,
> the 'empty' one in which the 'transmissions' occur ('O das
> Neue, Freunde, ist nicht dies') . . . , please paste over it at
> once this *Child's-Spring-Song,* written today, which better
> enriches the sound of the whole and stands not badly,
> as a pendant, opposite the offering to the white horse. . . .
>   This little song here, as it came to me today when I awoke,
> quite finished up to the eighth line, the rest following im-
> mediately, seems to me like an interpretation of a 'Mass'—
> a real *Mass,* gaily accompanied as with hanging garlands
> of music: the convent children sang it to I know not what
> text, but in this dance-step, in the little convent church at
> Ronda (in South Spain—), sang it, one can hear, to tam-
> bourine and triangle!—It fits, doesn't it, if one so wishes,

into those continuities of the Sonnets to Orpheus: as the brightest spring-tone in them? (I believe so.)

(Does the paper about match? I hope it is the same.)

Only this—and only because that XXIst is like a blot on my conscience.

One of the only two notes Rilke published with the *Sonnets* refers to this inspiration by the music of the dancing convent children at Ronda. The rather pedantic and obvious poem which this sonnet replaces has since been included in *Späte Gedichte* (p. 97).

Sonnet 23

This poem was apparently not one of those set down in the "single breathless act of obedience," but was added afterwards —"at least temporarily," Rilke wrote when sending a copy of it to Frau Knoop (March 18, 1922).

Sonnet 25

Like its counterpart, II, 28, this sonnet is addressed to Vera. Frau Knoop writes that Vera exclaimed shortly before she died: "Now I shall dance!"

Sonnet 26

Orpheus in his mourning ignored the Thracian women, who then, in revenge for his indifference, tore him to pieces in their Dionysian feasts. His head and his lyre were said to have been thrown into the river Hebrus and carried to the sea, to the shores of Lesbos.

In the postclassical phase of Greek culture, Orpheus was closely linked with Dionysus, into whose worship he was supposed to have introduced order and beauty.

Second Part

Sonnets 2 and 3

Mirrors are important in Rilke's imagery. The Second Elegy is perhaps of particular interest in this connection, with its angels, the early-fulfilled, like

> mirrors that draw their own outstreamed
> beauty into their own face again.

In the late poem "Narcissus" (*G.W.*, III, 415) Rilke describes that youth whose beauty is forever evaporating from him (again the Second Elegy) so that, though he would linger and be here,

> . . . all my boundaries are in a hurry,
> plunge out from me and are already yonder . . .

> What is reflected there and surely like me,
> and trembles upward now in tear-blurred lines,
> might perhaps come to being in some woman
> inwardly; it was not to be reached,

> no matter how I struggled towards it in her.
> It lies open now in the indifferent
> scattered water, and I may gaze on it
> at length under my wreath of roses. . . .

> . . . Narcissus passed away. From his beauty
> unceasingly arose his being's nearness,
> concentrated like the scent of heliotrope.
> But for him was set, that he should see himself.
>
> He loved what went forth out of him
> into himself again . . .

A *luster* is a chandelier with prismatic glass pendants, such as one would find in the great baroque halls; and a *sixteen-pointer* is a stag with sixteen points to its antlers.

Sonnet 4

In Malte's notebooks Rilke describes the last scene of the tapestry of the Lady with a Unicorn—"one of those tapestries that praise all and prostitute nothing"—(*G.W.*, V, 156; *A.W.*, II, 111):

> But here is yet another festival; no one is invited to it. Expectation plays no part in it. Everything is here. Everything for ever. The lion looks round almost threateningly: No one may come. We have never yet seen her weary; is she weary? or has she merely sat down because she is holding something heavy? A monstrance, one might say. But she curves her other arm towards the unicorn, and the flattered animal bridles and rears and leans against her lap. It is a mirror that she holds. See: she is showing the unicorn its likeness—.

Following his comment on "allusion," quoted in our foreword, Rilke goes on to say:

So too in the Unicorn no accompanying parallel with Christ
is meant; only all love for the not-proved, the not-tangible,
all belief in the worth and reality of that which our spirit
has through the centuries created and exalted for itself, may
be praised in it.

Sonnet 5

In a poem composed in Capri (letter to Countess Manon zu
Solms-Laubach, February 16, 1907) occur the following lines:

> . . . so we too can close
> at evening like the anemones,
> shutting into themselves depth of a day,
> and, something bigger, open again at morning.
> And to do this is not alone allowed us;
> this it is we must do: learn to close
> over what is infinite . . .

while Lou Andreas-Salomé (*Rainer Maria Rilke,* p. 66) quotes a
letter of June, 1914, in which Rilke says of himself:

I am like the little anemone I once saw in the garden in
Rome, which had opened so far during the day that it could
no longer close at night! It was dreadful to see it in the dark
meadow, wide open, how it still absorbed into its seemingly
frantically torn open calyx, with so much too much night
above it, and would not be done. And beside it all its clever
little sisters, each gone shut through its little measure of
abundance. I too am turned so helplessly outward, hence
distraught too by everything, refusing nothing, my senses
overflowing without asking me to every disturbance; if there
is a noise, I give myself up and *am* that noise, and since

everything once adjusted to stimulation wants to be stim-
ulated, so at bottom I want to be disturbed and am so with-
out end . . . [which explains] why all kindness of people
and of Nature remains wasted on me.

Sonnet 6

Rilke's note:

The rose of antiquity was a simple 'eglantine', red and yel-
low, in the colors that appear in flame. It blooms here, in
the Valais, in certain gardens.

The eglantine, more commonly known to us as the sweetbrier,
has single flowers.

Anyone who knows Rilke's work even slightly will scarcely
need to be reminded of his partiality for the rose. The inscription
on his gravestone reads:

> Rose o sheer contradiction desire
> to be no one's sleep under so many
> lids

Sonnet 8

Rilke's young cousin, Egon von Rilke, belonged, as he wrote
his mother (January 24, 1924, in Carl Sieber's *René Rilke*, p. 59),
to his "most unforgettable memories," and he goes on to say:

I think of him often and keep returning to that figure of
him which has remained indescribably moving to me. Much
'childhood', that which is sad and helpless in being a child,
is embodied for me in his form, in the ruff he wore, his
little neck, his chin, his beautiful brown eyes disfigured by a

squint. So I evoked him once more in connection with that eighth sonnet which expresses transience, after he had in his time served in the 'Notebooks of M. L. Brigge' as model for the little Erik Brahe, who died in childhood.

Rilke's note:

The lamb (in pictures) which speaks only through its inscription-bearing scroll.

Sonnet 11

According to the second of the only two notes Rilke published with the *Sonnets,* this poem refers

to the way in which, following an old hunting custom in certain regions of the Karst, the peculiarly pallid grotto-pigeons are scared out of their subterranean abodes by means of sheets carefully hung into their caves and suddenly swung in a particular manner, in order that they may be killed in their terrified escape.

Rilke became acquainted with the Karst, or Carso, the region forming the hinterland of Trieste, and famous for its miles of limestone caverns, during his stay at Duino Castle in 1912.

Sonnet 12

A literal translation of *den erkennt die Erkennung* should perhaps read "him Recognition recognizes," or might be rendered, as in Mr. Leishman's version of the *Sonnets,* "he is discerned by Discerning"; neither of these seems to cover quite the breadth of "apprehension by the understanding" I take to be implicit in Rilke's phrase.

Daphne, pursued by Apollo, it will be remembered, was transformed by her father, the river-god Peneus, into a laurel.

Sonnet 13

In writing Frau Knoop about the composition of the Second Part of the *Sonnets* (March 18, 1922), Rilke enclosed this one poem,

> because to *me* it is the nearest in the whole series and, perhaps, altogether the most valid one in it.

The Eighth Elegy closes with the picture of ourselves, like one turned on the last hill and lingering to look once more on all his valley—

> thus we live and are always taking leave.

The second quatrain of this sonnet brings to mind the lovely "Orpheus. Eurydike. Hermes" (1904; *Neue Gedichte, G.W.,* III, 99–102; *A.W.,* I, 181–184), an excellent translation of which by Stephen Spender appeared in *New Verse,* No. 5 (October, 1933).

Sonnet 16

The closing reference to the wisdom of dumb creatures (again the *Elegies,* and again the Eighth) seems to be drawn from the response of certain domestic animals to the custom of belling—a custom still prevalent in some communities of foreign origin in our own country—and reminds one of Kuoni's cow, in the first scene of Schiller's *Wilhelm Tell*, which will not eat if her bell is not about her neck.

Sonnet 19

Rilke's impressions of the beggars and other strange figures that so troubled his Paris days are recorded in Malte's notebooks, in his letters, and in various poems, particularly *The Voices* (*Die Stimmen*, in *Das Buch der Bilder, G.W.*, II, 119-132; included in the present translator's *Translations from the Poetry of Rainer Maria Rilke*, 1939, 110–128).

Sonnet 20

As far back as 1901, discussing marital problems, we find Rilke writing (to Emanuel von Bodman, August 17) that

between even the closest human beings infinite distances continue to exist.

Sonnet 22

In the second stanza Rilke is undoubtedly recalling the great bell in the Kremlin's campanile of Ivan the Great, built by Boris Godunov in 1600, which he had heard at Easter, 1900 (as he reminds Lou Andreas-Salomé in March, 1904); and the Column of Taharka (25th Dynasty), which he had seen towering over the remains of its fellows in the forecourt of "that incredible temple-world" at Karnak, by the light of a moon just beginning to wane: "one cannot take it in", he writes his wife (January 18, 1911), "it stands out so above and beyond one's life".

Sonnet 23

    Rilke's note: "To the reader".

    (See also the note on Rilke's relation to dogs, I, 16.)

Sonnet 25

    Rilke calls this

    the counterpart to the little Spring Song among the songs of the First Part of the Sonnets,

meaning I, 21.

Sonnet 26

    Lines 12–14: see note to I, 26.

Sonnet 28

    Rilke's note: "To Vera".

Sonnet 29

    Rilke's note: "To a friend of Vera's." (To himself?)